FORMED BY GOD: SPIRITUAL FORMATION IN A DISTRACTED AGE

Servant of CHRIST

Disclaimer

This book is a work of spiritual and theological reflection. While it draws extensively from Sacred Scripture and the historic Christian tradition, it is not intended as a substitute for pastoral counsel, sacramental life, or personal spiritual direction. Readers are encouraged to seek guidance appropriate to their individual circumstances.

Library of Congress Control Number (LCCN): 2026900835

Scripture Acknowledgements

Unless otherwise noted, Scripture quotations in this book are taken from the Revised Standard Version, Catholic Edition (RSV-CE). Copyright © 1966, 2006 by the Division of Christian Education of the National Council of the Churches of Christ in the United States of America. Used by permission. All rights reserved.

Where deuterocanonical texts are referenced, they are drawn from the Catholic biblical tradition.

Doctrinal Note

This work draws upon Sacred Scripture and the historic Christian spiritual tradition. While shaped by Catholic theology, it seeks to serve all Christians who long for deeper formation in Christ and a life faithfully lived in response to grace.

Publication Information

ISBN: 979-8-9945326-0-7
Printed in the United States of America

CONTENTS

CHAPTER ONE

THE CRISIS OF SPIRITUAL DISTRACTION

WE LIVE IN AN AGE UNLIKE ANY BEFORE IT—an age where distraction has become the ambient atmosphere of daily life. Noise surrounds us constantly. It fills our homes, shapes our thoughts, enters our relationships, and even follows us into the sacred space of prayer. Silence feels foreign. Stillness feels uncomfortable. Attentiveness to the voice of God feels increasingly rare. Modern life conditions us to be everywhere except fully present, and to hear everything except the whisper of the Holy Spirit. Our souls are bombarded with information, images, opinions, notifications and expectations that fragment our attention and scatter our focus across countless lesser things.

Yet distraction does not simply interrupt us; it forms us. It does not merely steal attention—it shapes desire. It dulls spiritual perception. It displaces God from the center of our internal gaze. Jesus understood this dynamic when He taught, **"The eye is the lamp of the body. So, if your eye is sound, your whole body will be full of light."** (Matthew 6:22). The "eye" represents the focus of the heart—our inner attention, our gaze, our meditation. When the eye is clouded by noise and cluttered by distraction, the entire interior life becomes dim. A fractured focus produces a fractured soul. And when the heart is divided among many competing lights, it can no longer receive illumination from the True Light who alone brings clarity, direction, and life.

This quiet spiritual erosion does not usually happen through sudden rebellion. It occurs gradually—almost imperceptibly—through distraction. Spiritual drift often begins with small compromises, tiny allowances, and unexamined habits. The believer rarely awakens one morning far from God;

1

instead, they drift one unguarded moment at a time. We can fill our lives with spiritual content—sermons, devotionals, worship music—yet slowly lose intimacy with God, not because we deny Him, but because we cannot hear Him above the noise. When Elijah stood on Mount Horeb, God was not in the wind, nor the earthquake, nor the fire, but in **"a still small voice"** (1 Kings 19:11–12). That is still His way with His children. The God who speaks in whispers requires a people who know how to be still.

The enemy understands this better than most Christians do. Satan does not need to destroy you to defeat you—he only needs to distract you. A distracted Christian is a spiritually powerless Christian. In Eden, the serpent began not by attacking Eve's identity but by shifting her attention. Scripture tells us, **"So when the woman saw that the tree was good for food, and that it was a delight to the eyes, and that the tree was to be desired to make one wise, she took of its fruit and ate; and she also gave some to her husband, and he ate."** (Genesis 3:6). Her downfall began with her gaze. What captured her eye eventually captured her desire. Likewise, what repeatedly captures your attention will eventually shape your affections. This is why spiritual distraction is not primarily a time-management issue; it is a warfare issue. The battleground of spiritual formation is the battleground of attention, and the enemy wants your gaze.

This constant distraction also slowly exhausts the soul. Many believers today feel weary—not only physically, but emotionally, mentally, and spiritually. They find themselves drained, scattered, overwhelmed, and unable to rest. Yet the root of this exhaustion is not simply overwork; it is overstimulation. A divided heart cannot experience peace. A scattered mind cannot discern the voice of God. A distracted spirit cannot receive strength. We were not created for ceaseless noise. Human beings were formed to walk with God in the cool of the day (Genesis 3:8), to dwell in His presence, to find rest and renewal through communion with Him. But the pace and pressure of modern life pull us away from this divine rhythm. As a result, we live constantly connected and yet spiritually depleted.

This is why Scripture urges us to **"lay aside every weight, and sin which clings so closely, and run with perseverance the race that is set before us,"** (Hebrews 12:1). Not every weight is sinful, but many weights are spiritually suffocating. Some distractions appear harmless, perhaps even good — but they drain the soul of focus and clarity. Spiritual formation often begins, not with addition, but with subtraction—with identifying and laying aside the unnecessary weights that pull our hearts away from Christ.

But distraction does more than scatter the mind. Its greatest danger is that it slowly steals desire. Distraction numbs holy hunger. It dulls spiritual longing. It makes everything except God seem urgent. A Christian may still believe in God intellectually yet feel distant from Him emotionally. Prayer becomes difficult, not because God is far but because the heart is preoccupied. Worship feels shallow, not because God is absent but because desire has been displaced. Scripture reading becomes dry, not because the Word lacks power but because the soul lacks stillness. This is the crisis of spiritual distraction: the slow erosion of desire for the presence of God. And desire—holy longing—is one of the first casualties of a noisy heart.

As distraction increases, spiritual shallowness follows. A generation trained by constant stimulation now struggles to sit with God long enough to be transformed by Him. The ancient practices that shaped the saints— silence, solitude, meditation, fasting, contemplation, unhurried Scripture reading—often feel uncomfortable or even impossible. But spiritual depth cannot be microwaved. Intimacy with God cannot be rushed. Formation requires patience, presence, and prolonged attention. The distracted believer learns to skim life, faith, Scripture, and even prayer. But God forms His people not in haste, but in depth. If the enemy cannot make us rebellious, he will make us restless. If he cannot make us corrupt, he will make us crowded. If he cannot destroy us, he will distract us. A crowded heart has no room for Christ.

Yet, in the midst of this crisis, God is issuing a profound and beautiful invitation. Even as noise surrounds us, He is calling His people back to stillness. Even as distraction increases, He is stirring fresh hunger. Even as attention fragments, He is inviting us into deeper communion. God is awakening His sons and daughters to the necessity of silence, focus, and spiritual attentiveness. The crisis is real—but so is the invitation. God is not overwhelmed by the noise of this age. He is not intimidated by the restlessness of the human heart. He still whispers. He still calls. He still draws near to those who will draw near to Him.

You were not created to live fragmented.
You were not created to live hurried.
You were not created to live spiritually numb.

You were created to live attentive to God, formed by His presence, and anchored in His peace. You were created to carry the stillness of heaven into the noise of earth. You were created to reflect the clarity and wholeness that comes from a heart centered on Christ.

The first step toward spiritual formation is simple yet profound: honest recognition. The courage to say before God, "My soul is distracted—but You are calling me deeper." Transformation does not begin with trying harder; it begins with reorienting the heart. Christian formation is not about self-improvement—it is about divine alignment. It is the Spirit of God shaping us into the likeness of Christ as we open our hearts, slow our pace, and surrender our attention to Him. This book will guide you into practices that quiet external noise, reorder internal chaos, and restore the soul to communion with God. It will help you recognize the subtle patterns of distraction that weaken your interior life and teach you how to cultivate rhythms of silence, surrender, Scripture, and spiritual discernment.

Spiritual formation is not only possible in this noisy age—it is essential. God is ready to shape you. He is ready to speak to you. He is ready to awaken holy desire within you. He is ready to transform you from the inside out. And it all begins here: with reclaiming the gaze of your heart and offering it back to the One who alone can satisfy it.

Closing Prayer

Eternal Father,

I come before You with a heart that is often scattered, divided, and pulled in many directions. I confess the ways I have allowed noise, hurry, and distraction to dull my desire for You. I acknowledge how easily my gaze drifts to lesser things and how quickly my attention fragments in the pressures of daily life.

Lord, reclaim the gaze of my heart. Restore within me a holy hunger for Your presence. Quiet the internal noise that competes with Your voice. Teach me to recognize the subtle ways distraction weakens my soul. Open my eyes to the weights I carry that You never intended me to bear. Where desire has grown numb, awaken longing again. Where my heart has been divided, make it whole. Where my spirit has been restless, anchor me in Your peace. Jesus, You are the True Light. Turn my eyes back toward You. Form my interior life so that my attention, affection, and desire are centered on You alone. Holy Spirit, draw me closer. Shape me through stillness, obedience, and communion. Let the whisper of Your voice become more real to me than the noise of the world.

Father, I surrender my distracted soul into Your hands. Make my heart undivided, my spirit attentive, and my life wholly Yours.

In Jesus' name, Amen.

CHAPTER TWO

THE FORGOTTEN DISCIPLINE OF STILLNESS

STILLNESS IS ONE OF THE OLDEST AND MOST SACRED spiritual disciplines in the history of God's people, yet it has become one of the most forgotten in our generation. In an age defined by noise, speed, and constant stimulation, stillness can feel unnatural—almost threatening. The modern soul has been conditioned to move quickly, respond instantly, and fill every moment with activity or distraction. Silence feels like wasted time; stillness feels like inactivity. But in the Kingdom of God, stillness is not inactivity—it is intimacy. It is not weakness—it is wisdom. It is not passivity—it is spiritual strength.

The divine invitation to stillness is not a polite suggestion; it is a command from the heart of God Himself: **"Be still, and know that I am God"** (Psalm 46:10). In this single sentence, God reveals both the posture we must take and the revelation He desires to give. Stillness is the doorway to knowing Him—not merely knowing about Him, but encountering Him, recognizing His voice, and experiencing His presence deep within the soul. God hides some of His richest treasures behind the veil of stillness. Only when the heart slows, when striving ceases, and when noise begins to fade, does the believer become capable of receiving the depth of what God desires to reveal.

Stillness, therefore, is not just stopping; it is surrender. It is not emptiness; it is openness. It is the intentional quieting of the soul so that

God Himself may fill it. Stillness is the practice of releasing control, of laying aside frantic activity, of refusing to let life's pressures dominate the interior life. It is the discipline of returning repeatedly to the truth that God is God—and we are not.

For thus says the Lord God, the Holy One of Israel: **"In returning and rest you shall be saved; in quietness and trust shall be your strength."** (Isaiah 30:15). In a world that measures strength by productivity, speed, and accomplishment, God defines strength in terms of quietness and trust. Stillness is not withdrawal from battle; it is a strategic positioning of the heart under the protection and leadership of God. This is why, when Israel stood before the Red Sea with the Egyptian army behind them, God spoke through Moses and said, **"The Lord will fight for you, and you have only to be still."** (Exodus 14:14). Stillness was not avoidance, it was deliverance. It was the posture through which God Himself moved.

Stillness trains the believer in the humility of dependence. It teaches the heart to confess, "God is in control, not me. God knows the way, not me. God fights the battle, not me." Stillness breaks the illusion of self-sufficiency. It confronts the pride that believes everything depends on our effort and reminds us that victory is found in surrender. It is far easier to act than to wait, far easier to strive than to trust, far easier to speak than to listen. But spiritual strength is found not in striving but in surrender. Stillness reorders the soul by returning it to its proper posture—resting under the sovereignty, wisdom, and leadership of God.

But if stillness is the doorway to God's presence, then noise is the barrier that blocks it. Noise is more than audible sound. It is anything—internal or external—that competes with the voice of God. Fear is noise. Anxiety is noise. Ambition, comparison, pressure, distraction, and hurried thoughts—all of these create internal static that mutes the whisper of the Holy Spirit. The enemy does not need to fill your life with sin to separate you from God; he only needs to fill it with noise. Noise distorts clarity, drowns discernment, and desensitizes the heart. We do not miss God because He is silent; we miss Him because we are loud. God whispers because He wants lovers, not spectators—hearts that lean in, not hearts that merely observe.

Stillness creates the environment where the presence of God becomes tangible. There are dimensions of His nearness that cannot be accessed while the soul is rushing, multitasking, or distracted. There are revelations that only emerge when the heart settles. There are encounters with God that simply do not happen until the believer chooses to slow down. In stillness, the believer becomes aware of the gentleness of the Spirit, the weightiness of God's presence, the stirring of conviction, the warmth of divine comfort, and the clarity of God's whisper. Stillness softens the heart that noise has hardened. It awakens holy desire that distraction has dulled. It restores sensitivity where busyness has produced numbness.

To be still is to allow God to breathe again into the weary places of the soul. Jesus promised His disciples a peace that the world cannot give: **"Peace I leave with you; my peace I give to you; not as the world gives do I give to you. Let not your hearts be troubled, neither let them be afraid."** (John 14:27). This peace does not depend on circumstances. It does not rise and fall with the conditions of life. It is rooted in the unchanging presence of Christ. Paul describes this peace as surpassing all understanding and guarding the heart and mind (Philippians 4:7). Stillness is the means through which we receive that peace. It is the sacred space where burdens are released, anxieties are surrendered, and the soul finds rest in God alone. The world offers escape, distraction, and temporary relief—but God offers rest. True rest. Transformational rest. Rest that renews the soul from the inside out.

Yet this kind of stillness does not appear magically. It must be cultivated intentionally, guarded diligently, and practiced consistently. The modern believer will never simply "find" time to be still—they must make time. It may begin with five minutes of silence, with a single moment of intentional breathing, with a short pause before God at the beginning or end of the day. Even these small pockets of stillness, practiced faithfully, can reshape the interior life. This is not legalism; it is formation. It is the relational invitation of a God who longs to be with His people. Stillness is not empty space; it is sacred space—space God fills with His presence.

As stillness becomes a rhythm of life rather than an occasional practice, the soul begins to experience its fruit. Anxiety loosens its grip, peace rises like a quiet tide, discernment sharpens, desires purify. The mind grows clear, the heart grows steady, the presence of God becomes more easily recognized. Stillness forms the spiritual core of the believer. It strengthens the interior life to resist temptation, hear God's guidance, remain steady in trials, and walk in step with the Spirit. A still heart becomes a discerning heart. A calmed spirit becomes a Spirit-led spirit. Stillness lays the foundation for spiritual transformation by giving the Holy Spirit room to work deeply within us.

In a world obsessed with hurry, God invites His people to slow down. He is not found in the rush; He is found in the quiet. He is not discovered in distraction; He is discovered in stillness. He is not revealed to the frantic; He is revealed to the surrendered. Stillness is not the absence of God—it is the environment where God becomes most present. When the believer slows down—truly slows down—God becomes clearer, His voice becomes recognizable, His love becomes felt, His presence becomes real.

Stillness is the pathway back to communion. Stillness is the posture of encounter. Stillness is the rhythm of the spiritually formed life. And in a world where everything moves faster, where noise feels inescapable, and where distraction has become the norm, stillness becomes not only a discipline—but a lifeline. It is the place where the believer meets God again, hears God again, and is restored by God again.

Closing Prayer

Lord God,

You who speak in whispers and reveal Yourself in stillness, I come before You, desiring the quiet that allows my heart to know You more deeply. In a world of noise, busyness, and constant motion, teach me again the sacred discipline of being still.

Father, quiet my soul. Silence the noise within me—fear, anxiety, pressure, comparison, and striving. Help me to release the illusion of control and rest fully in Your sovereignty. You have said, "Be still, and know that I am God." Today, I choose that posture. I choose surrender over striving and trust over anxiety. Lord, train my heart in the rhythm of holy stillness. Let my spirit become tender to Your presence, sensitive to Your whisper, and open to Your leading. May Your peace, which surpasses all understanding, guard my heart and mind in Christ Jesus.

Jesus, breathe order into my chaos, and renewal into my interior life. Holy Spirit, meet me in the silence. Restore the parts of me that noise has numbed and busyness has hardened. Shape my soul in the quiet so that I may walk with You in clarity, peace, and strength.

Lord, let stillness become my sanctuary— the place where I encounter You, the place where I am formed by You, the place where I am made whole again.

In Jesus' name, Amen.

CHAPTER THREE

CULTIVATING A LISTENING HEART

ONE OF THE GREATEST PRIVILEGES of the Christian life is the ability to hear the voice of God. The God who created the universe, who spoke worlds into existence, who upheld the patriarchs and guided the prophets, who walked with fishermen and called ordinary people into extraordinary purpose, is a God who still speaks today. He is not distant. He is not silent. He is not indifferent. He is a speaking God—one who reveals, guides, convicts, comforts, and communes with His children through His voice. Hearing God is not the inheritance of a spiritual elite; it is the birthright of every believer. Jesus declared, **"My sheep hear My voice, and I know them, and they follow Me"** (John 10:27). To belong to Christ is to be capable of recognizing His voice. Yet many Christians struggle not because God is quiet but because their hearts have not been trained to listen. Spiritual listening is not automatic, it must be cultivated, developed, guarded, and intentionally formed over time.

The real challenge is not God's silence but the noise of modern life. The heart is often filled with competing voices—fear, ambition, insecurity, culture, temptation, past wounds, and even the enemy's accusations. These voices crowd the interior life and drown out the gentle whisper of God. Noise does more than distract; it distorts. A noisy soul cannot discern. A hurried soul cannot hear. A crowded heart cannot receive revelation. Even Jesus, who lived in perfect communion with the Father, often withdrew to quiet places to pray (Luke 5:16). If the Son of God needed stillness to cultivate intimacy, how much more do we?

The journey toward hearing God always begins with desire. Samuel said, **"Speak, Lord, for thy servant hears"** (1 Samuel 3:10), and in this simple posture he modeled what every listening heart must hold: nearness to God, humility before God, and availability to God. Samuel placed himself close to God's presence—sleeping near the Ark. He responded to God with the humility of a servant. And he offered availability, expressing a willingness to hear whatever God wanted to say. Listening begins not with technique but with longing. Desire opens the ear of the soul. God speaks most clearly to those who genuinely want to hear Him and who approach Him with surrendered intention. A listening heart is a humble heart—one that believes God has something to say and is willing to respond when He does.

Learning to recognize God's voice is an ongoing process, shaped over time by the rhythms of Scripture, prayer, silence, and obedience. God speaks through His Word—the most reliable and primary expression of His voice. He speaks through the Holy Spirit—through conviction, internal promptings, impressions, and whispered guidance. He speaks through godly counsel—wise voices that echo the truth of Scripture. He speaks through circumstances—opening and closing doors, aligning opportunities according to His will. He speaks through peace—the inward confirmation of the Spirit. He may speak through supernatural encounters—visions, dreams, or unusual moments of clarity. And He speaks through the inner witness—a deep knowing that aligns perfectly with the character and truth of God. Jesus did not say merely that His sheep hear His voice; He said they know His voice (John 10:27). Knowing implies familiarity. Familiarity develops through repeated exposure, attentiveness, and responsiveness.

Yet several barriers hinder the development of a listening heart. Busyness replaces intimacy and suffocates discernment. When activity becomes a substitute for encounter, the inner ear of the spirit grows dull. Sin numbs the conscience, making the heart insensitive to the Spirit's leading. Fear speaks loudly, often overpowering God's gentle whisper; fear imagines worst-case scenarios while God speaks truth. Distraction fragments attention, making it impossible to focus long enough to hear God meaningfully. Unbelief silently closes the door of expectation—a heart that does not expect God to speak rarely recognizes when He does. And impatience prevents spiritual hearing, because God refuses to shout over noise or hurry. He waits until the heart slows. Spiritual formation requires dismantling these barriers and cultivating interior space where God's voice can be recognized and received.

Listening to God is not an event but a lifestyle. It is formed slowly, intentionally, and consistently through daily rhythms. A listening heart begins with silence before Scripture—pausing before reading, asking God to speak, reading slowly, and allowing the Word to examine the heart rather than rushing through it. Listening deepens through stillness in prayer—not filling every moment with words but allowing space for God's response. It is strengthened through journaling, which captures impressions, Scriptures, and recurring themes that reveal how God is shaping the interior life. Listening grows through small daily moments of quiet—five minutes of intentional silence before the day begins, a pause at midday, or a moment of reflection before sleep. Listening expands through asking God questions and expecting Him to answer in His way and time. The listening life requires active engagement, not passive waiting.

But listening is incomplete without obedience. Quick obedience, that is —responding quickly to God's promptings, no matter how small, always sharpens hearing. When God knows we will respond, He entrusts us with more revelation. Jesus did not say, "My sheep hear My voice" alone; He added, **"…and they follow Me"** (John 10:27). Following is the fruit of listening. Revelation without obedience produces stagnation. But obedience produces transformation. When we obey God's voice—whether through Scripture, conviction, or spiritual prompting—we grow in faith, discernment, and intimacy. Jesus said, **"If you love Me, you will keep My commandments."** (John 14:15). Hearing God is a gift; obeying God is worship. Every act of obedience strengthens the ability to hear God more clearly because obedience aligns the heart with His will.

A listening heart is formed through consistency, stillness, Scripture, prayer, purity, sensitivity, surrender, and deep desire. It is a heart softened by God's presence, freed from the grip of noise, attentive to the whisper of the Spirit, and yielded to whatever God desires. The world trains the heart to react; God trains the heart to listen. The world conditions the mind to rush; God calls the mind to rest. The world pulls the soul toward distraction; God draws the soul toward communion. Spiritual formation is impossible without the cultivation of a listening heart. Transformation begins in attentiveness. Being formed by God begins with hearing God. When the heart learns to listen, Scripture becomes alive as the Spirit illuminates truth. Prayer becomes intimate as it shifts from monologue to dialogue. Obedience becomes joyful because it flows from relationship, not obligation. Discernment becomes sharp, guiding decisions with clarity and peace. Identity becomes secure as the voice of the Father silences the lies of the enemy. Fear loses its grip and peace stabilizes the interior life. The presence of God becomes tangible—near, familiar, and life-giving. A listening heart becomes a transformed heart—a heart that walks with God, follows God, and reflects the character of Christ. In a world filled with noise, the believer with a listening heart becomes a prophetic witness, attuned to heaven when the world is tuned only to chaos.

Closing Prayer

Eternal Father,

I come before You with a deep longing to know Your voice more clearly. You are a speaking God, and I thank You that You desire communion with me. Quiet the competing voices within me—fear, doubt, insecurity, and distraction—that drown out Your gentle whisper. Soften my heart so that I may become attentive to Your presence.

Lord, teach me to listen. Give me a heart that desires Your voice above every other voice. Give me the humility to receive, the discernment to recognize, and the courage to obey. Holy Spirit, sharpen my spiritual hearing. Form within me a spirit of stillness, a posture of surrender, and a readiness to respond. Let Your Word shape my thoughts, Your whisper guide my steps, and Your peace confirm Your leading. Jesus, I offer You my attention. Align my desires with Yours. Transform my interior life so that Your voice becomes the anchor of my soul. May my heart be tender, receptive, and available to You always.

In Jesus' name, Amen.

CHAPTER FOUR

THE SLOW WORK OF TRANSFORMATION

W E LIVE IN A CULTURE THAT DESPISES SLOWNESS. Speed has become its highest virtue. Everything around us is optimized for immediacy - instant communication, instant rewards, instant responses, instant gratification. We are conditioned to believe that fast is efficient, fast is superior, fast is success. And because spiritual formation occurs within this hurried environment, many believers subconsciously assume that the work of God in their lives should also be fast. We want God to move quickly, heal quickly, transform quickly, and resolve quickly. Yet the ways of God do not bow to the pressures of modern speed. God forms His people in a different rhythm—one that is deliberate, steady, deep, patient, and often painfully slow.

God works slowly because He works thoroughly. He transforms gradually because He transforms profoundly. He shapes souls the way He grows trees—quietly, steadily, seasonally, and often invisibly. A tree does not grow by straining; it grows by remaining rooted. Likewise, spiritual transformation does not emerge from frantic attempts to grow but from steady surrender and faithful abiding in Christ. The slow work of God is one of the greatest tensions in the Christian life, because humans crave breakthroughs while God desires deep change. Breakthroughs can come instantly, but deep change rarely does. And God cares far more about depth than speed, far more about holiness than hurriedness, far more about lasting transformation than temporary inspiration.

Many believers picture transformation as an event—a dramatic moment, a powerful service, a convicting sermon, a sudden encounter with the Holy Spirit. And indeed, God often begins transformation in a moment. But He rarely completes it in a moment. Saint Paul in his second letter to the Corinthians uses continuous language to describe God's work within us: **"And we all, with unveiled face, beholding the glory of the Lord, are being changed into His likeness from one degree of glory to another; for this comes from the Lord who is the Spirit."** (2 Corinthians 3:18). Transformation is not a single event but an ongoing unfolding of Christ's likeness within the believer. It is shaped in the secret place, deepened through surrender, refined through discipline, matured through testing, and strengthened through obedience. God forms character slowly because He is not interested in shallow change. He is committed to deep, holy transformation—change that reaches motives, desires, identity, vision, and the hidden architecture of the soul. If God were to transform us instantly, our wounds would reopen, our old thought patterns would return, and the habits of the flesh would reassert themselves. Instant change rarely lasts. But when God transforms slowly, He reshapes us into different people altogether—people capable of carrying His calling, stewarding His presence, and sustaining spiritual maturity over a lifetime. The slow work of God produces resilience, depth, and permanence.

Much of God's transformative work takes place in hiddenness—where no one applauds, where no spotlight shines, and where the world sees no progress at all. Hiddenness is God's workshop. It is the sacred space where He does His deepest work. When God seems silent, He is working. When God feels absent, He is forming. When God slows us down, He is strengthening us from within. A seed grows underground before it emerges above the soil. If you judged its progress by visibility alone, you would assume nothing was happening. But beneath the surface, roots are forming that will one day support fruit. Jesus said, **"I am the vine, you are the branches. He who abides in Me, and I in him, he it is that bears much fruit, for apart from Me you can do nothing."** (John 15:5). Fruitfulness is the result of abiding, not rushing. Visible transformation is always rooted in invisible formation.

This is why God so often prioritizes depth over speed. Humans pray, "Lord, change me quickly," but God is shaping us slowly into the fullness of Christ. Romans 12:2 does not tell us to be instantly transformed. It says, **"Be transformed by the renewal of your mind."** Renewal is progressive. It unfolds day by day, layer by layer, belief by belief. God takes His time because He is crafting something eternal. What He builds slowly cannot be shaken by storms, seasons, disappointment, temptation, or spiritual warfare. Quick change excites us, but slow change strengthens us. Quick change inspires crowds, but slow change forms disciples. When God changes you slowly, the work becomes unshakeable.

There are profound reasons why God prefers slow transformation. Slow transformation stabilizes identity. Fast change may stir emotional excitement, but slow change produces spiritual grounding. Slow transformation purifies motives; it separates genuine desire for God from the desire for emotional highs or external validation. Slow transformation deepens dependence. If growth came instantly, we would rely on ourselves. When growth is gradual, we learn to lean on God, to trust His timing, and to walk in His strength. Slow transformation builds maturity—wisdom, discernment, humility, endurance. These qualities cannot be accelerated; they require the long obedience of daily surrender. Slow transformation glorifies God, not the believer. When growth is immediate, we are tempted to take credit. When growth is gradual, we know it could only have been the work of God.

But embracing the slowness of transformation is not easy. Patience does not come naturally to us. We desire momentum, clarity, answers, and visible progress. Yet the process of transformation disrupts our preferred timeline. It exposes our illusion of control. It humbles our expectations. Many believers experience frustration at their slowness, discouragement at recurring struggles, confusion at delayed answers, and restlessness when progress seems invisible. But these tensions are not signs of failure— they are signs of formation. The discomfort you feel is the stretching of your soul as God shapes it into the likeness of Christ. Slow growth is strong growth. Slow growth is lasting growth. Do not despise slow progress; it is evidence that God is working in places deeper than you can see.

His transformation is subtle, cumulative, and almost imperceptible in the moment. It happens beneath the surface of daily obedience. True transformation often looks like choosing forgiveness again. Returning to prayer after distraction. Reading Scripture even when tired. Saying "no" to sin in small ways. Choosing honesty when lying feels easier. Showing kindness under pressure. Trusting God's timing when you want immediate answers.

Surrendering your will when you'd rather hold on. These small, unseen decisions—repeated continuously—shape the soul more deeply than the emotional intensity of a single encounter.

In seasons when transformation feels painfully slow, the heart asks, "Why am I not growing faster? Why is this temptation still appealing? Why does this struggle persist? Why does God feel slow?" In these moments, you must remember: God is patient with your process. Be patient with yourself. The Potter never rushes the clay. He knows exactly what pressure, what shaping, what timing, and what environment are needed for transformation. God is not disappointed by your pace, He is committed to your formation. He works through your weakness, your wounds, your fears, and your inconsistencies. Nothing about your journey frustrates Him. You are not delaying Him. You are not too slow for Him. You are being molded according to His perfect timeline—not yours.

Saint Paul writes that we are being transformed **"from one degree of glory to another"** (2 Corinthians 3:18). Notice what the Scripture does not say. It does not say from weakness to glory. It does not say from brokenness to glory. It does not say from failure to glory. It says from one degree of glory to another. This means transformation does not begin from deficiency; it begins from grace. You are already standing in glory—the glory of salvation, the glory of being chosen, the glory of being beloved, the glory of being indwelt by the Spirit. And from that glory, God leads you to greater glory. You are progressing, even when you cannot see it. You are growing, even when you feel stagnant. You are pleasing to Him even as He forms you. Transformation is not a journey of shame but a journey of grace.

To embrace the slow work of transformation is to surrender to God's pace, His wisdom, His timing, His methods, and His unfailing love. Your timeline is not God's timeline. Your expectations are not God's expectations. But His timing is perfect, His methods are flawless, and His process is full of mercy. Surrender the need to hurry your growth. Release the pressure to be further along. Trust the God who is forming you with infinite patience. You are not behind. You are not late. You are exactly where God wants you to be. And the God who began this slow, beautiful work in you will be faithful to complete it.

Closing Prayer

Eternal Father,

I surrender myself to Your timing, Your process, and Your gentle, patient work within me. Teach me to release my desire for speed and to trust the rhythm of transformation You have ordained for my life. Quiet the restlessness within me that demands instant results and help me embrace the truth that lasting change takes time.

Lord, root me deeply in Your presence, form me slowly but thoroughly. Shape my character and strengthen my soul beneath the surface where only You can see. Give me patience when growth feels slow, give me hope when progress seems invisible and give me faith to believe that You are working, even when I cannot feel it. Jesus, renew my mind daily. Transform me from the inside out. Lead me from glory to glory as I abide in You. Holy Spirit, guide every quiet decision, every small surrender, every unseen act of obedience that shapes my heart into the image of Christ. May I rest in Your pace, trust in Your wisdom, and yield to Your love. Father, complete the good work You have begun in me. Make my transformation deep, lasting, and glorifying to You.

In Jesus' name, Amen.

CHAPTER FIVE

ORDERING THE INTERIOR LIFE

EVERY BELIEVER LIVES IN TWO WORLDS: the outer world of activity and responsibility, and the inner world of thought, desire, emotion, and spiritual posture. The outer world is visible—fast-moving, demanding, measurable, and often chaotic. But the inner world moves quietly beneath the surface, hidden from view yet governing the entire direction of life. It is within this unseen realm that spiritual formation takes place. It is the inner world that God consistently seeks to shape, heal, and reorder.

Scripture reminds us that the outer life is simply an expression of the interior life. Outward behavior flows from inward formation. Words originate from thoughts. Actions reveal values. Habits arise from desires. Choices reflect belief. Everything external begins internally. This is why Proverbs instructs, **"Keep your heart with all vigilance; for from it flow the springs of life."** (Proverbs 4:23). The heart is the source from which life is lived. When the interior life is ordered, the outer life becomes steady, focused, and fruitful. But when the interior life is disordered, even the strongest believer finds themselves overwhelmed, reactive, unstable, or spiritually stagnant.

Ordering the interior life is not a matter of self-help, emotional regulation, or mere introspection. It is a deeply spiritual discipline— an intentional cooperation with the Holy Spirit as He reshapes the interior fabric of the soul. God is not simply interested in modifying behavior. He is not satisfied with external conformity or superficial righteousness. He desires transformation from the inside out. He desires wholeness. He desires that the believer's inner world reflect His truth, His beauty, and His presence.

In Scripture, the "heart" is not just a place of emotion but the command center of the entire interior life. It encompasses the mind—thoughts, interpretations and reasoning. It includes emotions, reactions and sensitivities. It extends to the desires—longings, appetites, motivations. And it touches the will—the capacity to choose, obey, surrender, and respond. When Scripture speaks of the heart, it speaks of the whole inner person. And this whole person must be shaped, guarded, healed, and ordered by God. A misaligned heart leads to a misaligned life. A disordered heart leads to disordered priorities. A wounded heart leads to wounded decisions. But a heart surrendered to God becomes stable, discerning, wise, peaceful, pure, anchored, joyful, and whole. It becomes fertile soil in which spiritual formation can take root. It becomes the womb from which Christlike character is born.

Ordering the interior life begins with inviting God into the hidden places—places most believers prefer to keep closed. David models this courageous posture when he prays, **"Search me, O God, and know my heart; try me, and know my thoughts; see if there is any wicked way in me, and lead me in the way everlasting"** (Psalm 139:23–24). In this prayer, David opens the deepest corners of his being to the scrutiny of God. He invites divine light into hidden motives, buried wounds, secret fears, suppressed desires, unconscious habits, unprocessed grief, and unhealed memories. True spiritual maturity is not the absence of inner struggle; it is the willingness to bring those struggles into the presence of God. The heart God can transform is the heart God is allowed to examine.

The first major work of ordering the interior life is the renewal of the mind. Transformation cannot occur without a reformation of thought. Paul instructs believers to be **"renewed in the spirit of your mind"** (Ephesians 4:23). The mind is the battlefield where spiritual formation is won or lost. Thoughts shape beliefs, beliefs shape values, values shape decisions, and decisions shape destiny. If the mind is filled with fear, impurity, lies, shame, or worldly thinking, the life will inevitably reflect that disorder. Renewing the mind involves replacing lies with truth, fear with faith, confusion with clarity, and worldly perspectives with biblical wisdom. This renewal is not instantaneous; it is continuous, daily, rhythmic. Just as the world constantly floods the mind with noise, images, and influences, Scripture must continually cleanse, anchor, and stabilize the interior

ORDERING THE INTERIOR LIFE

life. A renewed mind becomes a quiet mind. A quiet mind becomes a listening mind. A listening mind becomes a transformed mind.

But ordering the interior life also involves the healing of emotions—an aspect of formation many believers have neglected or misunderstood. Emotions are not enemies; they are indicators. They point to deeper realities within the soul. Emotions reveal where healing is needed, where lies have taken root, where fear lives, where shame hides, where wounds remain, and where God desires to restore. Jesus Himself displayed deep emotional life—grief, compassion, sorrow, righteous anger. God is not intimidated by human emotions. He longs to heal them, refine them, and align them with His truth. Ordering the emotional life does not mean suppressing feelings or pretending they do not exist; it means bringing them honestly into the presence of God. When emotions are healed, the interior life becomes fertile ground for formation.

Ordering the interior life also requires the purification of desires—perhaps one of the deepest and most transformative aspects of spiritual formation. Desire is powerful. Every sin begins with desire. Every act of obedience flows from desire. Every calling is carried by desire. This is why Psalm 37:4 says, **"Delight yourself in the Lord, and He will give you the desires of your heart."** This does not mean God grants every wish; it means He transforms desire itself. As believers delight in Him, He reshapes what they long for. He purifies what they pursue. He sanctifies their inner appetites. Spiritual formation is not merely behavior modification—it is desire transformation. When desires are purified, holiness becomes joyful, worship becomes natural, prayer becomes a longing rather than a duty, obedience becomes peaceful, and the allure of sin fades in the light of Christ's beauty.

But perhaps the most central aspect of ordering the interior life is surrendering the will. The will is the hinge upon which the soul turns. Every act of obedience or disobedience begins with a decision of the will. And Jesus gave the ultimate model of surrendered will when He prayed, **"Not my will, but Yours be done"** (Luke 22:42). This is the foundation of all spiritual formation. Surrender is not weakness—it is worship, it is alignment, it is liberation from the tyranny of self. A surrendered will becomes a willing will—willing to obey, willing to trust, willing to follow, willing to release control even when the flesh resists. God never forces transformation; He invites it. And the will must respond.

As the Holy Spirit begins ordering the interior life, a pattern emerges—a rhythm of four movements that repeats throughout the believer's journey. First, illumination: God reveals what is out of order. Second, surrender: the believer yields that area to God. Third, renewal: the Spirit replaces old patterns with new truth. And fourth, formation: the heart, mind, desires, and will come into greater alignment with Christ. These movements happen again and again— through seasons, through trials, through silence, through breakthroughs. Ordering the interior life is not a one-time achievement; it is a lifelong rhythm of surrender and renewal.

When the interior life becomes ordered, the entire life changes. The believer becomes stable and anchored. Anxiety loses its grip, discernment sharpens, spiritual hunger increases, obedience becomes joyful, sin loses its access points, relationships begin to heal, peace becomes consistent, prayer becomes deeper, worship becomes richer and above all the presence of God becomes tangible in daily life. But when the interior life is disordered, small problems feel overwhelming, fear multiplies, sin gains footholds, confusion clouds decisions, purpose becomes uncertain, and the presence of God feels distant. God longs to reorder the interior life because He desires His people to be whole—emotionally, mentally, spiritually, and relationally. A spiritually formed believer is not a perfect believer; they are a reordered believer—one whose inner world has been rearranged according to the truth, wisdom, and beauty of Christ.

Closing Prayer

Eternal Father,

I surrender my heart to You—the thoughts I hide, the emotions I bury, the desires I fear, the wounds I avoid, and the patterns I cannot change on my own. Search me, Lord. Shine Your light into every hidden corner of my mind. Reveal what is broken, what is misaligned, what is wounded, what is resistant, and what is longing for Your touch.

Renew my mind with Your truth. Heal my emotions with Your compassion. Purify my desires with Your holiness. Strengthen my will with Your Spirit. Jesus, reorder my interior life according to Your beauty and Your wisdom. Shape my heart so that everything within me aligns with Your will. Teach me to guard my heart, to dwell in Your presence, and to live from the inside out.

Holy Spirit, continue Your gentle work in me—illumining what needs to change, inviting surrender, renewing my mind, and forming me into the image of Christ. Let my interior life reflect Your peace, Your purity, and Your presence.

In Jesus' name, Amen.

CHAPTER SIX

WHEN SCRIPTURE BECOMES YOUR ATMOSPHERE

Spiritual formation is impossible apart from the living and active Word of God. Scripture is not supplemental to the Christian life—it is foundational. It is the lamp that illuminates the path, the truth that confronts deception, the food that nourishes the soul, the sword that pierces darkness, and the gentle rain that softens the heart. Every dimension of spiritual growth—healing, renewal, transformation, discernment, maturity—flows from a life deeply rooted in Scripture. Without the Word, the believer becomes spiritually malnourished and emotionally unstable, easily swayed by culture, circumstances, and personal impulses. Jesus affirmed this when He declared, **"Man shall not live by bread alone, but by every word that proceeds from the mouth of God"** (Matthew 4:4). Bread sustains the body, but the Word sustains the soul. Without Scripture, the interior life slowly suffocates.

In an age of distraction, Scripture immersion has become not merely important but essential. Many believers read Scripture occasionally, but few immerse themselves in it. There is a vast difference between exposure to the Word and immersion in the Word. Exposure glances at Scripture; immersion lingers in it. Exposure informs the mind; immersion transforms the heart. Exposure reads a verse quickly before rushing into the day; immersion allows the verse to read *you*. Immersion means slowing down, absorbing truth, praying through passages, meditating deeply and inviting the Holy Spirit to illuminate.

David captured the essence of Scripture immersion when he wrote, **"I have laid up Your word in my heart, that I might not**

sin against You" (Psalm 119:11). Hidden does not mean "glanced at"; it means stored, treasured, internalized. Immersion is not about the speed of reading but the depth of abiding. Transformation through Scripture rarely occurs in hurried reading; it emerges through prolonged saturation. The believer who immerses themselves in Scripture becomes grounded, discerning, stable, and spiritually alert. Scripture is not merely a historical record or theological textbook; it is the primary vocabulary of God's voice. A believer who desires to hear God clearly must fill their heart with His Word. Scripture trains the inner ear to recognize His voice, corrects emotional impulses, protects against deception, clarifies decision-making, and deepens intimacy with the Spirit. Saint Paul's instruction, **"Let the word of Christ dwell in you richly..."** (Colossians 3:16), reveals God's intention—that Scripture would not visit us occasionally but saturate us abundantly. A Scripture-rich believer becomes a Spirit-sensitive believer.

One of the most neglected disciplines in modern Christian life is biblical meditation. Meditation is not emptying the mind but filling it with Scripture until the heart burns with divine truth. Joshua 1:8 commands believers to meditate on the Word "day and night" so that they may walk wisely and prosper spiritually. Saint Alphonsus Liguori teaches in his book *Attaining Salvation* that meditation bears fruit when it moves the will toward God. Reading Scripture prepares the heart, but it is holy affections; acts of humility, trust, detachment, surrender, love, and repentance—that unite the soul to Him. Meditation, therefore, is not completed in reflection, but in the loving response of the heart.

The work of Scripture is not completed in understanding alone, but is further strengthened through contemplative prayer—a form of prayer that moves beyond words into silent, loving awareness of God. In contemplative stillness, the Scriptures you've read begin to breathe within you; verses become encounters, truths become experiences, and the presence of God rests gently on the soul. Contemplation draws the Word from the mind into the inner chambers of the heart, where it can heal wounds, purify motives, calm anxiety, and awaken holy affection. When meditation and contemplation flow together, they create an interior environment where Scripture can take root and reshape the entire interior life.

Yet Scripture does not only comfort; it also confronts. Immersion requires allowing the Word to expose what is misaligned within us. Scripture is a mirror that reveals hidden motives, a sword that divides truth from deception, and a fire that purifies desires. Hebrews 4:12 teaches that the Word "discerns the thoughts and intentions of the heart." This is why Scripture sometimes stings before it heals—it reveals before it restores. Transformation requires truth, and truth often confronts first. But confrontation in Scripture is never condemnation. The Spirit convicts to heal, reveals to restore, and exposes to transform. God wounds pride so He can build humility. He dislodges lies so He can anchor truth. He challenges sinful patterns so He can form Christlike character.

Scripture immersion is not meant to be a task, a duty, or a religious performance. When Scripture becomes obligation, it loses its power to form us. But when Scripture becomes communion with God—relational, conversational, interactive—transformation flows naturally. Paul did not instruct believers to study Scripture occasionally; he said Scripture must "dwell" in us, settle in, inhabit the soul, fill the atmosphere of the heart. Immersion is not about reading more but about receiving more—being formed by the living Word until Christ is reflected in thought, desire, emotion, and action.

As believers immerse themselves in Scripture, the Word begins to reorder reality from the inside out. It reorganizes thinking by dismantling false beliefs and building a foundation of truth. It reshapes desire by weakening unhealthy cravings and strengthening holy longing. It stabilizes emotion by calming anxiety, weakening fear, strengthening hope, and grounding the heart in peace. It reforms choices by sharpening discernment, guiding decision-making, and making obedience joyful rather than burdensome. Scripture immersion also reorders identity, enabling the believer to see themselves through the eyes of God rather than through shame, insecurity, or cultural distortion. Through the Word, the believer becomes anchored in Christ—rooted, confident, and secure.

For Scripture to shape the interior life, it must surround the believer. Immersion requires atmosphere, not just moments. It means praying Scripture, journaling Scripture, listening to Scripture, memorizing Scripture, displaying verses in daily environments, studying slowly, rereading repeatedly, meditating deeply, and inviting the Holy Spirit to illuminate. When Scripture becomes the atmosphere you breathe, its influence flows into every part of your life—your thoughts, habits, relationships, passions, and decisions.

31

A life immersed in Scripture bears unmistakable fruit. It becomes stable during storms, discerning in confusion, peaceful under pressure, wise in decision-making, bold in calling, and pure in desire. The believer becomes rooted in truth, grounded in God's character, and anchored in spiritual identity. The Word becomes their lamp, compass, shield, bread, anchor, sword, wisdom, and strength. Scripture immersion rewrites the inner world with divine truth and trains the soul to live in alignment with the voice, nature, and purposes of God.

In a noisy world, Scripture becomes the quiet strength of the believer. In a confused culture, Scripture becomes clarity. In spiritual dryness, Scripture becomes refreshing water. In emotional instability, Scripture becomes steady ground. In temptation, Scripture becomes armor. In suffering, Scripture becomes comfort. Immersion in the Word is how the believer remains rooted in Christ and formed by the Spirit. It is not an optional practice—it is the lifeblood of a spiritually formed life.

Closing Prayer

Eternal Father,

Your Word is life to my soul, truth to my mind, and light to my path. I thank You for the gift of Scripture—alive, powerful, and able to transform me from within. I come before You asking not merely to read Your Word, but to be shaped by it, saturated in it, and transformed through it.

Holy Spirit, open the eyes of my heart, Illuminate the Scriptures as I read. Let truth penetrate deeply, let Your voice rise clearly and let Your presence rest upon every word. Lord, confront every lie within me, uproot every false belief, purify every desire and heal every wound that Your Word reveals. Make Scripture my atmosphere, my comfort, my clarity, my strength. Let it dwell richly within me until Christ is formed in every part of my interior life. Jesus, You are the Living Word, shape me through Your written Word so I may reflect Your heart, think Your thoughts, and walk in Your ways.

Father, anchor me in Scripture, that I may become rooted, steady, discerning, and deeply formed in You.

In Jesus' name, Amen.

CHAPTER SEVEN

THE REFINING FIRES OF TRIALS

S PIRITUAL FORMATION DOES NOT UNFOLD only in peaceful moments, beautiful encounters, or quiet mornings with God. While those experiences nurture the soul, they are not the primary places where the deepest formation occurs. Many of the most significant transformations of the human heart happen in the furnace of hardship—in the griefs we did not choose, the disappointments we did not expect, and the pressures we did not invite. Trials are uncomfortable, disruptive, and often painful. Yet in the mysterious wisdom of God, they become sacred classrooms, refining fires through which He shapes His people into the likeness of Christ.

Though trials rarely feel holy, they produce holiness. Though they rarely feel like kindness, they are instruments of God's love. And though they do not feel like God drawing near, they often reveal His nearness more vividly than any blessing can. Saint James, in a striking opening to his letter, writes, **"Count it all joy, my brethren, when you meet various trials, for you know that the testing of your faith produces steadfastness."** (James 1:2–3). Joy—not because the pain is pleasant, but because the purpose is profound. Trials are not signs of divine neglect; they are often invitations into deeper intimacy, deeper trust, and deeper transformation.

Comfort hides many things in the human heart. In seasons of stability and ease, we can overlook unhealthy attachments, unquestioned assumptions, small compromises, and fragile places of faith. Comfort can numb us, distract us, or make us overlook areas of our hearts that need healing. But trials reveal what comfort conceals. A trial exposes what we truly trust, where our hope is anchored, what idols still influence us, what lies still shape our thinking, and where fear quietly governs our emotions. Trials reveal the condition of the soul not to shame us, but to heal us. God cannot transform what we refuse to acknowledge, and He often uses pain to bring buried issues to the surface so He can deal with them tenderly.

Saint Peter writes that trials come **"So that the genuineness of your faith, more precious than gold which though perishable is tested by fire, may redound to praise and glory and honor at the revelation of Jesus Christ"** (1 Peter 1:7). Gold is purified in fire; impurities rise, are removed, and the metal becomes stronger and more beautiful. In the same way, trials purify faith. They burn away self-reliance, illusions of control, false confidence, and shallow thinking. They strengthen the believer with a faith that can withstand pressure, temptation, and spiritual attack. You do not know the strength of your faith until it is tested. You do not know the faithfulness of God until you must rely on Him desperately. You do not know the nearness of God until everything else falls away. Trials become training grounds where trust is formed, deepened, and proven.

Trials are not random events drifting into the believer's life. They are purposeful instruments in the hands of a loving God. He uses trials to strengthen faith, produce endurance, purify motives, deepen surrender, increase compassion, teach obedience, and prepare His children for their assignments. Every calling has a stretching; every purpose requires refinement. God wastes no pain. Even when the purpose is hidden, the work is holy.

Much of the transformative work of suffering happens beneath the surface. During a trial, you may feel spiritually stagnant, emotionally drained, or unable to discern any progress. Yet beneath those feelings, God is quietly at work—deepening your roots, stretching your capacity, healing hidden wounds, purifying your intentions, sharpening your discernment, and strengthening spiritual muscle. The growth that happens in suffering is often invisible until the season shifts. Only when you look back do you realize how much God built in you while you felt weak, weary, or confused. It is often after the fire that you realize, "I am not who I was before this trial." You find new stability, deeper humility, stronger compassion, wiser discernment, and a richer awareness of God's presence. Trials grow you in ways comfort never can. They strip away the superficial and make room for what is eternal.

Though trials feel lonely, God is never absent in them. Scripture presents a consistent picture of a God who steps into the fire with His people. He was with Joseph in the pit and prison, with Daniel in the lions' den, with the three Hebrew men (Hananiah, Mishael and Azariah) in the furnace, and with Jesus in Gethsemane. Trials have a way of revealing "Emmanuel"—God with us—in ways blessings never do. The furnace becomes a place of encounter. The trial becomes a place of revelation. Hardship becomes a place where the presence of God becomes undeniably real. The fire you face is not evidence of God turning away from you; it is often the place where He walks closest beside you.

Trials also play an essential role in forming character. Romans 5:3–4 teaches that **"More than that, we rejoice in our sufferings, knowing that suffering produces endurance, and endurance produces character, and character produces hope."** Christlike character is not formed in comfort. It grows through stretching, endurance, and the experience of God's faithfulness in difficulty. Trials teach humility, patience, endurance, compassion, wisdom, integrity, spiritual depth, and holy fear. These virtues cannot be learned through teaching alone—they must be forged.

Trials not only reveal the believer's weakness; they reveal God's strength. In suffering, believers discover God's sustaining grace, His unshakeable sufficiency, His comforting presence, His peace in chaos, His wisdom in confusion, His companionship in loneliness, and His power in weakness. Job, after unimaginable suffering, declared, **"I had heard of You by the hearing of the ear, but now my eye sees You"** (Job 42:5). Trials move believers from hearing about God to encountering God. They shift knowledge from conceptual to experiential. They take God from the periphery of life to the center of it.

Every trial has a purpose, and every fire has an end. Trials are temporary, though they may feel endless. But formation is eternal. The fruit of trials outlives the trial itself. God uses suffering to produce enduring transformation—rooting believers deeply in His love, stabilizing their hearts in His truth, and preparing them to carry the weight of their calling with humility and strength. God does not lead His people into fire to abandon them; He leads them through the fire so that when they emerge, they carry a faith that is purified, resilient, and radiant.

37

Trials form a kind of beauty that ease cannot create. They forge a depth of wisdom, a tenderness of compassion, a steadiness of soul, and an intimacy with God that cannot be gained through any other means. The refining fires of trials are not barriers to spiritual formation; they are catalysts. They do not hinder transformation; they accelerate it. They are not evidence of God's displeasure; they are His tools of preparation. God is not merely trying to make our lives easier—He is forming our souls. He is shaping us into the likeness of His Son, who Himself learned obedience through suffering (Hebrews 5:8). The path of formation is not a path of comfort but a path of surrender, endurance, and deeper trust. And in every trial, the believer is invited to discover God more intimately, trust Him more deeply, and reflect Him more clearly.

Closing Prayer

Eternal Father,

I come before You with the trials that press upon my heart—the ones I understand, and the ones I do not. I confess that suffering often feels confusing, painful, and overwhelming. Yet I also acknowledge that You are the God who works all things together for my good, even when the path is difficult.

Lord, refine me through every fire, purify my faith, strengthen my endurance, cleanse my motives, deepen my surrender and form Christ within me. Jesus, walk with me in the fire as You walked with Hananiah, Mishael and Azariah. Let me sense Your nearness more than the heat of the trial. Let Your presence be my peace, my strength, and my assurance.

Holy Spirit, reveal what You want to heal, transform, and restore within me. Give me eyes to see Your work beneath the surface. Give me grace to persevere, patience to trust, and courage to remain faithful.

Father, let this trial not be wasted, use it to shape me, mature me, and draw me nearer to You. And when the season ends, may I emerge with a faith that is stronger, a heart that is purer, and a life that reflects Your glory.

In Jesus' name, Amen.

CHAPTER EIGHT

THE WAR FOR YOUR THOUGHTS

EVERYTHING THAT SHAPES THE SOUL.—every emotion, every desire, every habit, every action—first passes through the realm of thought. Thought is the birthplace of spiritual formation. The battle for spiritual maturity is not fought externally, but in the hidden chambers of thought. God transforms His people by transforming how they think. Defeated thinking produces defeated living. Impure thinking darkens the soul even when outward behavior appears righteous. Anxious thinking chokes out peace. Cynical thinking smothers hope. Fearful thinking paralyzes faith. The person formed in Christ must learn not only how to pray, worship, and serve, but how to think—how to separate God's voice from internal noise. How to recognize lies, how to cultivate truth, and how to resist the subtle influences that shape the mind away from God. 2 Corinthians 10:5 reveals both the intensity and intentionality required for this battle: **"We destroy arguments and every proud obstacle to the knowledge of God, and take every thought captive to obey Christ,"** This is not passive language—it is warfare language. Taking thoughts captive means not allowing every idea that enters your mind to settle. It means refusing to allow them roam freely, influence your emotions, or shape your identity. You become a gatekeeper—evaluating thoughts, interrogating them, comparing them to the truth of God, and deciding whether they deserve a place in your interior life. You cannot stop thoughts from entering, but you can decide what remains. The spiritually formed mind learns to ask: Does this thought align with God's character? Does it reflect truth? Does it produce peace or confusion? Does it build faith or fear? Does it draw me toward Christ or away from Him?

41

A mind given freedom to drift will drift toward fear, shame, comparison, or fantasy. Minds do not drift toward holiness—they must be set on truth intentionally. Setting the mind means choosing what you will meditate on. It is an act of spiritual responsibility, not emotional reaction. The mind must be anchored deliberately in what is eternal, not what is temporal; in what is true, not what is persuasive; in what is holy, not what is entertaining. The life formed in Christ requires mental discipline as much as it requires prayer or worship. The enemy does not gain influence over the believer by overpowering their spirit; he gains influence by planting suggestions. He whispers through fear, memory, imagination, comparison, assumptions, insecurities, and distorted interpretations. He does not need the believer to openly rebel; he only needs them to agree with a thought that contradicts the truth of God. Thoughts become agreements, agreements become beliefs, beliefs shape desires, and desires shape destiny. This is spiritual warfare at its most intimate level: the invisible interior struggle for the agreement of the soul. This war for your thoughts is subtle. The enemy rarely announces his presence, he does not argue loudly; he suggests quietly. He does not shout lies; he frames them as possibilities. He does not overwhelm with force; he influences with deception. He aims not to control your intellect, but to distort your perception of God, yourself, and your circumstances. Every battle you face externally begins internally with a thought: a suggestion to fear, a whisper of inadequacy, a memory of shame, a lie about God's heart, or a distorted interpretation of reality. Victory or defeat grows from that beginning point.

Thoughts are seeds. A single thought, if planted, can become a belief. If believed, it becomes an attitude. If nurtured, it becomes a desire. If acted upon, it becomes a habit. If repeated, it becomes a stronghold. If unchallenged, it forms identity. A thought becomes a lens through which life is interpreted. This is why Scripture commands believers to renew, guard, set, discipline, and focus the mind. The mind left unguarded becomes vulnerable ground for lies, but the mind renewed by truth becomes a fortress of spiritual strength.

Saint Paul writes about "strongholds"—invisible chains made of repeated lies that feel true even when they are false. These may sound like "I will always be afraid.", "I will never change.", "I am inadequate.", "God is disappointed in me.", "My past defines me.", "This sin is stronger than I am." A stronghold is not simply a wrong thought; it is a lie that has been believed for so long it begins to feel like reality. But strongholds do not fall by willpower; they fall by truth. Jesus said, **"and you will know the truth, and the truth will make you free"** (John 8:32). Truth is not merely informational—it is liberational. It breaks chains. When a lie is confronted with Scripture, its power collapses.

But truth must be identified, embraced, and meditated upon to overturn the long-standing patterns of the mind. Demolishing strongholds require discernment to identify the lie, courage to confront it, humility to release it, and devotion to replace it with truth. The peace of God becomes the fruit of a mind that has learned to remain centered on Him. Peace does not emerge from perfect circumstances; it emerges from refusal to wander into fear or anxiety. A wandering mind produces instability; a stayed mind produces rest. When the mind continually returns to God's presence, God's character, and God's promises, peace flows even in the midst of chaos. Peace is not the absence of trouble; it is the inner stability produced by truth governing thought. Every believer has an inner dialogue—a constant stream of interpretation, reflection, judgment, memory, imagination, and self-talk. More spiritual formation happens in this inner dialogue than in external events. Your inner voice shapes how you see yourself, how you interpret your day, how you respond to challenges, how you perceive God, and how you make decisions. You must teach your inner voice to speak truth. You cannot allow shame, emotion, fear, or insecurity to narrate your story. Your soul must learn to echo God's truth within your own thoughts. Replacing lies with truth is the most practical act of spiritual warfare. Every lie has a corresponding truth from God. Lies bind; truth frees. Lies shame; truth restores. Lies distort; truth clarifies. Lies weaken; truth strengthens.

In his letter to the Colossians, Saint Paul gives another instruction: **"Set your minds on things that are above, not on things that are on earth."** (Colossians 3:2). To "set" the mind implies active choice—a deliberate focusing. Just as you set a compass or set your gaze upon a fixed point, you must set your mind on truth, purity, holiness, God's promises, Christ's character, and the hope of eternity. Setting the mind is not denial of earthly reality; it is anchoring the soul in eternal truth. What the mind sets itself upon, the soul begins to reflect.

Closing Prayer

Eternal Father,

I bring before You the hidden landscape of my mind—the thoughts I speak, the thoughts I suppress, the thoughts I fear, and the thoughts I struggle to control. You know every belief that shapes me, every lie that has wounded me, every fear that grips me, and every thought that has strayed from Your truth.

Renew my mind, Lord, rewrite my patterns of thinking, expose every lie I have believed, whether whispered by the enemy, formed in past wounds, or shaped by my own fears. Replace them with truth that sets me free. Holy Spirit, be the guardian of my thought life. Teach me to recognize what is not from You, give me discernment to reject deception and wisdom to embrace truth. Strengthen me to take every thought captive and make it obedient to Christ.

Jesus, steady me with Your peace, anchor me in Your presence, and shape me with Your truth until my thoughts reflect Your heart. Father, establish my mind in the truth of who You are, the truth of who I am in You, and the truth of Your promises that cannot fail.

In Jesus' name, Amen.

CHAPTER NINE

THE PRACTICE OF SACRIFICIAL SURRENDER

I F SPIRITUAL FORMATION HAS A CENTER—its heartbeat, its deepest work, its most defining posture—it is surrender. Surrender is where transformation begins, and it is where transformation continues. It is not a single emotional moment, not a dramatic spiritual milestone, and not a one-time decision made long ago. Surrender is a daily posture of the heart, a continual yielding of will, desires, fears, plans, and identity into the hands of God. It is the place where the soul stops striving to manage itself and begins to rest in divine leadership.

Surrender is often misunderstood. It is not God taking something from you; it is God freeing you from what binds you. It is not loss; it is alignment. It is not defeat; it is formation. Every step of spiritual growth you have encountered in this journey—stillness, listening, Scripture immersion, renewal of the mind, endurance through trials—has been preparing you for this: a life fully yielded to God. Scripture reminds us that God desires the heart before He desires action: **"My son, give Me your heart, and let your eyes observe My ways."** (Proverbs 23:26). And the heart is only truly shaped when it is surrendered.

At the core of surrender is the tension of two wills. Human beings are born with a deep desire for control. We want certainty, predictability, security, and outcomes we can manage. We want clarity before obedience and assurance before trust. Yet God invites us into a life that is not governed by control, but by trust. This creates an inner struggle—your will and God's will, pressing against one another. Even Jesus, perfect and sinless, faced this tension in

Gethsemane. He prayed with honesty and anguish, **"My Father, if it be possible, let this cup pass from me; nevertheless, not as I will, but as thou wilt."** (Matthew 26:39). That moment reveals something profound: surrender is rarely without struggle, surrender requires honesty, surrender demands trust, and surrender is never passive. It is an intentional act of faith. Jesus' surrender in Gethsemane led to our redemption on Calvary.

Surrender is difficult because it confronts the illusion of control—an illusion we cling to even when it quietly exhausts us. We hold tightly to our plans, preferences, interpretations, timelines, identities, and expectations. Often, these are not evil things, but they become barriers when they compete with God's leadership. Surrender touches the most tender areas of life: our anxieties, relationships, dreams, reputation, finances, comfort, wounds, and future. It exposes what we fear losing and reveals what we trust more than God. In this way, surrender becomes a mirror. It exposes idols we did not know we carried and false securities we leaned on without realizing it. But this exposure is not meant to shame us; it is meant to free us. Surrender transforms because it breaks the power of anything that competes for the heart.

The language Saint Paul uses when he speaks of surrender in Romans 12:1 is striking. **"I appeal to you therefore, brethren, by the mercies of God, to present your bodies as a living sacrifice, holy and acceptable to God, which is your spiritual worship."**. A living sacrifice is ongoing—it must be renewed daily, because the human heart has a tendency to reclaim control. A living sacrifice is also holistic. It is not merely spiritual devotion; it is the offering of the entire life—thoughts, desires, time, relationships, ambitions, resources, and identity. The surrendered life is not partly God's and partly yours; it is wholly His. Yet this wholeness is not restrictive, it is liberating.

True surrender reaches beyond what we dislike or fear, it also reaches into what we love most. Abraham's surrender of Isaac reveals this reality. God was not after Isaac's death; He was after Abraham's undivided heart. Surrender always touches desire. It brings into God's hands the things we cling to most tightly—the dreams we cherish, the futures we imagine, the identities we protect. God is not intent on stripping us of joy; He is intent on freeing us from attachments that distort joy. When desires are surrendered, God does not annihilate them; He purifies them and returns them transformed, aligned with His purposes and filled with deeper life. The work of surrender happens primarily within. It is an interior movement of letting go—releasing fear, control, self-righteousness, outcomes, timelines, the need to be understood, the need to be in charge, the need for comfort, and the false identities we construct to feel safe. Letting go is painful because it requires trust. Letting God lead feels risky because it removes our ability to predict or manage. Yet surrender creates interior spaciousness—room for the Holy Spirit to work freely, to speak clearly, to heal deeply, to redirect gently, and to form Christ within us. When our hands are clenched, we cannot receive. When our hands are open, God can fill them.

At its core, surrender is not driven by fear; it is driven by trust. To surrender is to say to God, "I trust Your wisdom more than my reasoning. I trust Your timing more than my impatience. I trust Your plan more than my desires. I trust Your love more than my fear." This kind of trust does not come from information alone; it grows from intimacy. The more deeply you know God's heart, the more confidently you place your life in His hands. Trust is the soil in which surrender grows. Sacrificial surrender touches every dimension of the interior life. It involves the surrender of the mind—allowing reasoning to submit to revelation, opinions to bow to truth, and assumptions to be corrected by God's Word. It involves the surrender of the heart—yielding desires to holiness, emotions to God's peace, and wounds to His healing. And it involves the surrender of the will—aligning choices with God's commands, allowing obedience to become immediate rather than delayed. When the mind, heart, and will move together in surrender, spiritual formation deepens and accelerates.

Uncertainty often becomes the environment where surrender is most clearly revealed. When clarity fades and life becomes unpredictable, the instinct is to grasp for control. Yet God uses uncertainty to draw His people closer, inviting trust one step at a time. Uncertainty exposes what we cling to and what we worship. In these seasons, surrender transforms uncertainty into intimacy. God does not always reveal the entire path; He reveals enough to invite trust in the next step. The believer who learns to surrender in uncertainty discovers a God who is present, guiding gently and faithfully moment by moment. There is a peace that cannot be experienced apart from surrender. This peace does not come from understanding every situation; it comes from releasing the situation into God's care. Control fuels anxiety but surrender releases it. As the grip of control loosens, the presence of God fills the space. The peace that flows from surrender is not fragile; it is steady and rooted in trust rather than circumstance. Fear weakens, striving ceases and the soul begins to rest.

Obedience becomes the visible evidence of surrender. One cannot claim surrender while resisting obedience. Surrender and obedience are inseparable. Obedience is surrender expressed in action, and surrender is obedience embraced in the heart. When you obey God even when it costs you, confuses you, or stretches you, you demonstrate that He truly has your heart. Obedience without surrender becomes legalism and surrender without obedience becomes illusion. True surrender produces a life that increasingly aligns with God's will. On the other side of surrender lies freedom— not freedom from responsibility, but freedom from inner bondage. Surrender releases the soul from fear, pride, anxiety, the need to control, the need to impress, the fear of people, emotional instability, and spiritual confusion. It lifts the burden of managing life and replaces it with trust in God's care. Beyond surrender is joy. Beyond surrender is clarity. Beyond surrender is transformation. Beyond surrender is peace.

Sacrificial surrender is not a moment reserved for crises or mountaintop encounters; it is a daily practice. Each day becomes an invitation to yield again: thoughts, desires, fears, plans, relationships, and will. This repeated yielding forms Christ more deeply within the soul. Surrender is not a loss of self; it is the discovery of the self God intended you to become. And as surrender becomes your way of life, spiritual formation moves from effort to grace, from striving to rest, and from control to communion.

Closing Prayer

Eternal Father,

I come before You with open hands and an open heart. I confess how often I cling to control, certainty, and my own understanding. I see how tightly I hold my plans, my fears, my desires, and my expectations. Today, I choose to release them to You, teach me to surrender—not in fear, but in trust. Help me yield my mind to Your truth, my heart to Your healing, and my will to Your wisdom.

Jesus, form in me a life of daily surrender. Free me from what competes with You. Purify my desires. Quiet my striving. Anchor my soul in Your love. Holy Spirit, show me where You are inviting deeper release. Give me the courage to let go, the faith to trust You fully, and the grace to obey joyfully.

Father, I place my life on the altar again today. Please receive it. Shape it. Transform it. And let my surrender become the place where Christ is formed most deeply within me.

In Jesus' name, Amen

CHAPTER TEN

LIVING IN THE PRESENCE OF GOD

THERE IS NO GREATER PRIVILEGE IN THE LIFE of a believer than the ability to live in the presence of God. Not merely to visit His presence during moments of prayer, worship, or gathered worship, but to abide in Him continuously— to live with a settled awareness of His nearness woven into the fabric of everyday life. Human beings were created for this kind of communion. Before sin fractured relationship, humanity walked with God freely, without fear, shame, or distance. Redemption through Christ did not only forgive sin; it restored access. It reopened the way into God's presence and invited humanity back into relational closeness, intimacy, and union with Him.

The heart of God has always been proximity. He does not merely call His people to serve Him from afar, but to walk with Him—to live their lives consciously aware that He is near. As Saint Paul declared, **"In Him we live and move and have our being"** (Acts 17:28). God's presence is not something we enter and exit; it is the environment in which we live. We do not visit God's presence—we dwell in it. Many believers think of God's presence as a place they enter into at specific times, but Scripture reveals something far more profound: God's presence is not something we visit; it is where we live. To live in God's presence is to recognize that every moment unfolds within Him. Life itself is sustained by His nearness.

There is a significant difference between visiting God's presence and dwelling in it. Visiting is occasional and inconsistent, shaped by circumstances and emotional states. Dwelling is steady, rooted, and continuous. Those who visit God's presence often experience spiritual highs and lows, fluctuating peace, and inconsistent intimacy. Those who dwell in His presence experience sustained peace, steady guidance, inner stability, resilience, and a quiet confidence rooted not in circumstances but in communion. When Jesus called His disciples to abide in Him, He was inviting them into a life of continual attachment, like a branch connected to a vine. The branch does not attach and detach; it remains. And in remaining, it receives nourishment, strength, and life.

Living in the presence of God begins with awareness. God's presence is never absent; the issue is never His nearness but our attentiveness. Awareness is the gentle, intentional acknowledgment that God is here—now, in this moment. It is cultivated not through strain but through remembering, pausing, breathing, and turning the heart toward Him. Sometimes a single whispered phrase is enough to restore awareness: "God, You are here. I am with You. Holy Spirit, I acknowledge Your presence." Awareness transforms ordinary moments into sacred ones. Washing dishes, driving, working, resting, walking, waiting—each becomes a place of encounter when the heart remembers God's nearness.

One of the greatest deceptions believers face is the idea that God is only present in explicitly "spiritual" moments. In truth, God is as present in the ordinary as He is in the extraordinary. The sacred is not limited to sanctuaries; it permeates daily life. Many believers do not lack God's presence—they lack awareness of it. God can be encountered in stillness and in movement, in silence and in speech, in joy and in ache. Every moment holds the potential for communion because every moment unfolds in God. Living in God's presence is not about achieving perfect attentiveness. Minds wander. Emotions drift. Attention fractures. What matters is not perfection but return. Formation happens in the habit of returning—again and again—gently, without condemnation, back to God's presence. The spiritual masters called this 'recollection': the frequent gathering of the heart back to God. You return with a breath, a whisper, a pause, a moment of silence. Over time, returning becomes instinctive, and awareness deepens naturally. What begins as effort becomes rest.

The presence of God is not only comforting; it is transformative. In His presence, fear loosens its grip, anxiety weakens, shame dissolves, identity stabilizes, desires are purified, and burdens lift. Scripture confirms this transforming power: **"Thou dost show me the path of life; in Thy presence there is fullness of joy, in Thy right hand are pleasures for evermore."** (Psalm

16:11). Transformation happens not primarily through striving, but through remaining. Moses did not reflect glory because of effort, but because of encounter; after dwelling in God's presence, **"the skin of his face shone"** (Exodus 34:30). Presence leaves a mark. Those who remain with God begin, slowly and quietly, to resemble Him. The soul that abides in God's presence is formed by Him. Rest is one of the clearest evidences of a life lived in God's presence. The soul that abides no longer strains to prove itself or hustles for worth. It stops striving spiritually and begins to rest. Rest is not merely a break from activity; it is the atmosphere of a heart held by God. In God's presence, rest becomes inner stillness, emotional quiet, mental peace, spiritual surrender, and the deep assurance of being loved. To dwell in God's presence is to live rested in His care. Awareness of God's presence also cultivates holiness. Not holiness driven by fear or legalism, but holiness shaped by love. When the heart lives aware of God's nearness, sin loses its appeal. Not because God threatens, but because intimacy transforms desire. Awareness purifies motives, speech, imagination, relationships, and choices. Holiness becomes the natural fruit of abiding, not the forced result of striving.

God's presence is also guiding. It is not static or passive. When a believer lives aware of God's nearness, guidance becomes subtle yet clear. Correction is gentle. Direction is quiet. Nudges are tender. Over time, the believer learns to sense God's pace, timing, and ways. His presence becomes a compass, leading not through loud commands but through inward peace and clarity. Living in the presence of God requires intentional rhythms that nurture awareness. Beginning the day in stillness before the world demands attention, whispering short prayers throughout the day that re-center the heart, taking sacred pauses between transitions, allowing Scripture to draw attention back to God's voice, and ending the day with reflection—remembering where God's presence was sensed and what stirred the heart. These rhythms do not create God's presence; they awaken awareness of it.

Spiritual formation reaches maturity in abiding. Not merely praying, but communing. Not merely seeking God, but staying with Him. Not merely experiencing His presence occasionally, but living within it. Jesus made this unmistakably clear: **"Apart from Me you can do nothing"** (John 15:5). Apart from this nearness, efforts produce no lasting fruits. But when a believer abides, life becomes quietly powerful. The heart that remains becomes a heart that resembles Christ. A life lived in God's presence becomes a life that reflects His glory—not through effort, but through nearness.

Closing Prayer

Eternal Father,

I thank You that You are near—closer than my breath, present in every moment of my life. Forgive me for the ways I forget, rush, or live distracted from Your nearness. Awaken my awareness, Lord. Train my heart to return to You gently and often. Help me recognize Your presence in the ordinary moments of my day.

Jesus, form me through nearness, not striving. Let Your presence quiet my fears, steady my heart, and purify my desires. Teach me to rest in You and to walk with You moment by moment. Holy Spirit, guide me from within. Draw my attention back when it wanders. Make my life an abiding place for God.

Father may my days be lived consciously before You, my heart anchored in Your presence, and my life shaped by continual communion with You.

In Jesus' name, Amen.

CHAPTER ELEVEN

ENCOUNTERING JESUS IN THE HOLY EUCHARIST

A T THE VERY HEART OF THE CHURCH'S LIFE stands a mystery so profound that words can only gesture toward its depth: the Holy Eucharist. Among all the gifts Christ left to His people, none bears such intimacy, humility, and transforming power. In the Eucharist, Jesus does not merely teach, inspire, or remind—He gives Himself. His Body. His Blood. His life offered as nourishment for weary souls. This gift fulfills His own promise: **"and lo, I am with you always, to the close of the age."** (Matthew 28:20). The Eucharist is not an idea to be contemplated from a distance; it is a mystery to be received with reverence and awe. It is not simply remembered; it is encountered at the celebration of the Mass.

When Jesus took bread and wine and spoke the words, **"This is My body… This is My blood"** (Matthew 26:26–28; Mark 14:22–24; Luke 22:19–20), He was not offering metaphor alone. He was revealing divine reality clothed in mystery. Scripture tells us that what Jesus speaks is truth and life (John 6:63). Christ gives Himself not because His sacrifice was incomplete, but because His love is inexhaustible. He feeds His people with His own life so that they may live in Him, just as He promised: **"He who eats My flesh and drinks My blood has eternal life, and I will raise him up at the last day."** (John 6:54). Few passages confront the listener as directly as Jesus' teaching in John 6. When He declared, **"Truly, truly, I say to you, unless you eat the flesh of the Son of man and drink His blood, you have no life in you"** (John 6:53), many were disturbed and turned away. Yet Jesus did not soften His words or call them back. Instead, He allowed the mystery to stand, revealing that true

55

life flows from union with Him. The Eucharist is not an accessory to that union—it is the sacramental means through which it is deepened. Christ was and is saying that His life must become our life, His sacrifice our strength, His presence our nourishment. To receive the Eucharist is to allow Christ to enter the innermost places of the soul. The Apostle Paul affirms this reality when he writes that the cup and the bread are a participation in the Blood and Body of Christ (1 Corinthians 10:16). This communion is not passive remembrance but active sharing. Paul further warns that the Eucharist must be approached with reverence, for it is truly the Lord's Body when he wrote **"For as often as you eat this bread and drink the cup, you proclaim the Lord's death until he comes. Whoever, therefore, eats the bread or drinks the cup of the Lord in an unworthy manner will be guilty of profaning the body and blood of the Lord."** (1 Corinthians 11:26–27). Such warnings only make sense if something sacred and real is being received. The Eucharist draws the believer into living communion with Christ Himself.

The Eucharist is not an isolated ritual disconnected from daily life. It is one of God's most powerful instruments of spiritual formation. Jesus Himself declared, **"As the living Father sent Me, and I live because of the Father, so he who eats Me will live because of Me."** (John 6:57). Each encounter nourishes the soul, heals interior wounds, purifies desire, strengthens faith, and anchors identity. Christ feeds the believer so that His life may be formed within them. Just as physical bread sustains the body, this heavenly bread sustains the soul.

Throughout the Church's history, believers have recognized that Christ is truly present in the Eucharist. This presence is not dependent on emotional experience but on Christ's promise and power. The risen Lord who revealed Himself in the breaking of the bread on the road to Emmaus continues to reveal Himself in that same breaking today. Hearts burn, eyes are opened, and faith is renewed—not because of ritual alone, but because Christ is present. Jesus did not institute the Eucharist for the spiritually accomplished. It is not a reward for perfection, but mercy for weakness. Christ came not for the healthy, but for those who know they need healing (Mark 2:17). The Eucharist is not reserved for those who feel worthy; it is given for those who know they need grace. It is food for wandering hearts, strength for tired souls, mercy for those who stumble, comfort for the grieving, and healing for the broken. At the

56

altar, Christ does not recoil from human frailty—He meets it with divine generosity. At its deepest level, the Eucharist is the sacrament of union. Jesus promised, **"He who eats My flesh and drinks My blood abides in Me, and I in him."** (John 6:56). This abiding deepens prayer, strengthens obedience, and forms Christ within the believer. Union with Christ is not abstract theology—it is lived reality, nourished repeatedly through this holy gift. Much confusion surrounds the idea of receiving the Eucharist "worthily." Scripture clarifies that worthiness does not mean sinlessness, but reverence and repentance (1 Corinthians 11:28), making the sacrament of reconciliation a vital prerequisite for receiving Christ in the Eucharist worthily. Jesus Himself gave the Church the sacrament of reconciliation when He said **"Truly, I say to you, whatever you bind on earth shall be bound in heaven, and whatever you loose on earth shall be loosed in heaven."** (Matthew 18:18). God desires a humble and contrite heart (Psalm 51:17), and such a heart finds healing at the altar.

The Eucharist also shapes the believer for mission. Having received Christ's self-giving love at the celebration of the Mass, the believer is sent to live that love in the world. Saint Paul reminds us that participation in one bread makes us one body. Communion draws believers together and sends them forth as witnesses of Christ's love, carrying His presence into the ordinary spaces of life. Every celebration of the Eucharist is also a foretaste of what is to come. Scripture points to the wedding feast of the Lamb (Revelation 19:9), where communion will be complete and unending. Each reception strengthens hope, reminding the believer that earthly formation prepares the soul for eternal union. The Eucharist sustains the journey and reveals the destination. To encounter Jesus in the Holy Eucharist is to encounter love made tangible, humility made visible, and grace made consumable. Christ does not remain distant. He comes near. He gives Himself fully. And through this holy mystery, believers are drawn ever deeper into the life of God— formed not by striving, but by communion.

Closing Prayer

Lord Jesus Christ,

You who give Yourself as living Bread from heaven, I come before You in awe and gratitude. You offer not something from Yourself, but Yourself entirely, for the life of my soul.

Teach me to approach the Holy Eucharist with reverence, humility, and hunger. Remove distraction and routine that dull my awareness of this sacred gift. Nourish my soul with Your life. Heal what is wounded within me. Purify my desires. Strengthen my will for holiness. May each encounter at the altar draw me deeper into union with You, shape me into Your likeness, and prepare my heart for eternal communion with You.

Amen.

CHAPTER TWELVE

BECOMING A PERSON OF ETERNAL DEPTH

A T THE HEART OF SPIRITUAL FORMATION lies a quiet yet demanding invitation: to become a person of eternal depth. This invitation is not to intensity, charisma, visibility, or performance. Depth is not something that can be displayed or measured outwardly; it is something the soul becomes over time as it is shaped by God. Scripture consistently points beyond what is seen to what endures, reminding us that **"we look not to the things that are seen but to the things that are unseen; for the things that are seen are transient, but the things that are unseen are eternal."** (2 Corinthians 4:18). Eternal depth is the quality of a life anchored beyond the present moment—rooted in God, oriented toward eternity, and formed by what lasts. Depth is revealed not in how loudly one speaks of faith, but in how firmly one is held by it. A person of eternal depth possesses an identity that remains stable regardless of circumstance. Their peace is not fragile or reactive. Scripture describes such a person as **"a tree planted by streams of water, that yields its fruit in its season, and its leaf does not wither. In all that he does, he prospers."** (Psalm 1:3). Depth produces resilience. It allows the believer to remain steady when conditions are harsh and when emotions fluctuate.

The modern world, however, trains the soul in the opposite direction. Speed is celebrated. Noise is constant. Surface-level engagement is rewarded. Scripture warns that such a life leaves the soul malnourished, describing people who are **"always learning and never able to come to the knowledge of the truth"** (2 Timothy 3:7). Superficial faith may survive ease, but it collapses under pressure. Jesus Himself warned in Matthew 13:20–21 that shallow roots cannot sustain life when trials come. God forms deep souls because only depth can carry weight—weight of suffering, obedience, love, responsibility, and glory. Scripture reminds us that God looks not at outward appearance, but at the heart (1 Samuel 16:7). Eternal depth develops where the heart is slowly and faithfully shaped by God, not hurried by culture. Shallow lives may appear strong, but they fracture easily. Deep lives may appear quiet, but they endure. A person of eternal depth is not defined by outward religious activity, but by inward transformation. Their identity is no longer shaped by comparison, approval, success, or failure, but by belonging to God. Scripture affirms this grounding truth: **"You are hidden with Christ in God"** (Colossians 3:3). Because identity is secure, emotional turbulence loses its authority. Depth is cultivated primarily in hidden places. Jesus spoke often of the value of what is done in secret—prayer, fasting, surrender—assuring that the Father who sees in secret will reward openly (Matthew 6:4–6). God forms souls away from applause and visibility, shaping character where no one else is watching. What God does in secret becomes the strength that sustains public life.

Becoming a person of eternal depth requires intentional choice. Depth does not happen accidentally. One must choose silence over constant noise, prayer over distraction, Scripture over endless entertainment, purity over compromise, surrender over self-will, eternity over immediacy, and presence over productivity. Depth requires pruning. God lovingly removes what is shallow in order to strengthen what is eternal. Much of what the world applauds is spiritually empty, while much of what heaven treasures remains unseen. The believer who chooses depth walks a narrow path, but it is a path that leads to life.

Yet depth cannot be produced by discipline alone. It is not the result of willpower or spiritual ambition. It is the work of the Holy Spirit. Scripture makes clear that transformation is God's work within us: **"It is God who works in you, both to will and to work for His good pleasure"** (Philippians 2:13). Spiritual formation is cooperation, not self-improvement. The believer offers availability and surrender; the Spirit brings lasting change. The person of eternal depth learns to live with eyes fixed beyond the visible. Life is no longer interpreted only through circumstances, emotions, or cultural pressure, but through eternal perspective. Suffering is not meaningless, waiting is not wasted, obedience is not burdensome, sacrifice is not loss, holiness is not optional, and death is not final.

When the unseen becomes more real than the visible, the soul is liberated from fear and driven by hope. The believer begins to invest in what will outlast them—truth, love, faithfulness, and obedience.

Ultimately, depth expresses itself through love. Scripture is unequivocal: love is the measure of maturity. 1 Corinthians 13:2 says, **"And if I have prophetic powers, and understand all mysteries and all knowledge, and if I have all faith, so as to remove mountains, but have not love, I am nothing.".** The deeper a person is rooted in God, the more their life becomes a steady outpouring of patient, truthful, sacrificial love. Love is not an accessory to formation; it is its fullest fruit. The soul formed deeply in God reflects His love naturally and consistently. As depth matures, the believer becomes a presence in the world. Not a performer, not a loud voice, but a steady, holy presence. Such a person calms rather than agitates, listens more than speaks, responds with wisdom, walks with gentleness, lives with conviction, and embodies Christ in ordinary moments. Their life becomes a sanctuary—a place where others encounter peace, safety, and hope. Depth is not dramatic. It is quiet, strong, steady, and enduring. And the world desperately needs people like this—souls anchored in God, unshaken by chaos, and formed by eternity.

Closing Prayer

Eternal Father,

I receive Your invitation to depth. Not a depth I can manufacture, but a depth You alone can form within me. I confess my attraction to what is shallow, quick, and visible, and I surrender again to Your slower, deeper, eternal work. Root my life deeply in You. Stabilize my identity in Your love. Quiet my soul with Your peace. Renew my mind with Your truth. Purify my desires and strengthen my will.

Holy Spirit, continue forming Christ within me. Prune what is shallow. Deepen what is eternal. Expand my capacity to love, to trust, and to endure. Teach me to live with eyes fixed on eternity, to value what heaven values, and to carry Your presence into every ordinary moment.

Father, make my life a sanctuary, my heart a dwelling place, and my soul a witness to the beauty of a life deeply formed in You.

In Jesus' name, Amen.

CHAPTER THIRTEEN

THE POWER OF OUR MOTHER'S INTERCESSION

ROM THE OPENING PAGES OF THE GOSPEL to the final moments at the foot of the Cross, the Blessed Virgin Mary stands quietly yet unmistakably at the heart of God's redemptive plan. Chosen by God's grace, overshadowed by the Holy Spirit, mother of the Savior, first disciple of Christ, and model of perfect surrender, Mary is not merely a figure of history. She is a living spiritual reality within the life of the Church. Scripture itself affirms that all generations will call her blessed because of what God has done through her (Luke 1:48). Her place in the Christian life is deeply relational, profoundly maternal, and inseparably connected to the mystery of Christ. Mary's role has always been singular and clear: she leads us to Jesus. Her life magnifies the Lord rather than herself, just as she proclaimed in her Magnificat: **"My soul magnifies the Lord, and my spirit rejoices in God my Savior"** (Luke 1:46–47). She never draws attention to herself for her own sake. Her presence directs us to obedience, her words orient us toward trust, and her intercession flows entirely from her union with her Son. When Jesus entrusted Mary to the beloved disciple from the Cross, He was not speaking symbolically or sentimentally. He was establishing a spiritual reality: **"Behold, your mother"** (John 19:27). In that moment, Christ gave His Church a mother—one who would intercede, guide, and accompany believers on their journey toward Him.

Mary's intercession does not compete with Christ's unique mediation; it flows from it. Scripture is clear that Christ alone is the one Mediator between God and humanity (1 Timothy 2:5). Yet

Scripture also reveals that God invites human participation in His saving work through prayer and intercession (James 5:16). Mary's intercession is powerful not because of her own authority, but because of her intimacy with Jesus. She prays because she loves Him, and He listens because He loves her. Her motherhood in grace is a gift of Christ's own heart, extended to His people in tenderness and mercy. The Wedding at Cana provides the clearest scriptural revelation of Mary's intercessory role. When the wine ran out—a moment of quiet crisis—Mary noticed. Before anyone asked, she perceived the need. She brought the situation to Jesus without instruction or demand, simply stating, **"They have no wine"** (John 2:3). Even when Jesus responded that His hour had not yet come, Mary remained confident. She turned to the servants and spoke words that have echoed through centuries of discipleship: **"Do whatever He tells you"** (John 2:5). Through her intercession, Christ performed His first sign, and His glory was revealed (John 2:11).

In Cana, Mary revealed the heart of her mission. She sees need. She intercedes. She trusts. And she leads others to obedience. This pattern remains unchanged. Mary's intercession always leads to Christ, never away from Him. Her prayers open space for grace, and her presence encourages faith-filled obedience. Cana is not merely a miracle story; it is a blueprint for how Mary intercedes for the Church. Mary's intercessory power does not arise from divinity, but from intimacy. She is powerful because she is close—to Christ's heart, to His suffering, to His mission, and to His love for humanity. She carried Christ in her womb, formed Him in silence, followed Him in faith, and stood faithfully at the Cross when others fled (John 19:25). Her intercession flows from this deep participation in the life and suffering of her Son. Mary's maternal heart is revealed in the way she intercedes. Scripture repeatedly presents motherhood as a place of tenderness, vigilance, and advocacy (Isaiah 66:13). A mother notices what others overlook. She carries burdens quietly. She stands beside her children when they fail. Mary is not a distant figure removed from human experience. She understands fear, uncertainty, suffering, and hope. Her intercession is maternal—marked by compassion, patience, and perseverance. Mary is also the Church's greatest model of spiritual formation. Her life embodies humility that receives God's word **("Behold, I am the handmaid of the Lord; let it be to me according to your word"** – Luke 1:38), trust that embraces the unknown, obedience without delay, and contemplation that treasures God's work in silence. Her fiat became the doorway through which Christ entered the world. This same posture of surrender lies at the heart of all spiritual formation. To walk with Mary is to learn how to receive Christ, how to carry Him within, and how to follow Him even when the path leads to suffering. There is a reason Scripture presents Mary as the woman whose obedience stands in contrast to Eve's disobedience (Genesis 3; Luke 1). There is a reason the enemy fears Mary. It is not because she possesses power apart from God, but because her humility crushes pride, her obedience reverses rebellion, her purity exposes corruption, and her surrender defeats self-will. Her "yes" allowed Christ to enter the world; her intercession continues to draw souls toward Him. God exalts the humble (Luke 1:52), and Mary's humility remains one of the enemy's greatest defeats. Throughout history, saints and spiritual giants have recognized her role in spiritual warfare, not as a rival to Christ, but as a humble servant whose presence magnifies His victory.

Mary's intercession shapes the spiritual life in countless ways. She teaches surrender without fear, perseverance through suffering, trust in silence, and obedience rooted in love. Scripture reveals her present with the early Church in prayer (Acts 1:14), reminding us that she continues to accompany believers as they await the work of the Spirit. She strengthens faith when it feels weak, encourages hope when shame weighs heavily, and gently leads hearts back to Jesus. To walk with Mary is to experience the Christian journey accompanied by a mother's care. She guides gently, patiently, and faithfully through seasons of confusion, trial, waiting, dryness and renewal. Just as she accompanied Jesus from Bethlehem to Calvary, she accompanies the Church on its pilgrimage toward glory. Her presence does not replace Christ's; it deepens our experience of Him. Mary is not the destination of the journey—Christ alone is. But she is the mother who walks beside us toward Him, echoing her timeless instruction: **"Do whatever He tells you"** (John 2:5). In her intercession, believers find encouragement. In her motherhood, they find refuge. And through her guidance, they are led ever more deeply into the heart of Christ.

Closing Prayer

Blessed Mother Mary,

Given to us by your Son as a gift of love, I come to you with the trust of a child. Teach me to listen, to surrender, and to obey as you did. Pray for me, Mother, when my faith grows weak, when my heart grows weary, and when my path becomes unclear. Intercede for me as you did at Cana— seeing what I lack and bringing it quietly before Jesus. Lead me always to your Son. Help me to say *yes* to God's will, to stand faithfully in times of trial, and to trust even when I do not understand.

Holy Mother of God, form Christ within me through your prayers. Guard my heart, strengthen my faith, and guide me gently toward deeper union with Jesus.

Amen.

CHAPTER FOURTEEN

FASTING AND THE REORDERING OF DESIRE

AT THE DEEPEST LEVEL, THE SPIRITUAL LIFE is not shaped by information alone, but by desire. What the soul longs for ultimately determines how it lives. Desire directs attention, fuels decisions, shapes habits, and forms identity. Scripture consistently affirms this inner reality: **"Where your treasure is, there your heart will be also"** (Matthew 6:21). This is why spiritual formation is never merely about changing behavior; it is about reordering the heart. Fasting enters precisely at this point, as one of God's most profound tools for reorienting desire.

Fasting is often misunderstood as a harsh discipline focused on deprivation. In reality, fasting is not primarily about what is removed, but about what is revealed. Scripture describes fasting as a humbling of the soul before God (Psalm 35:13). When the body is denied what it regularly relies upon, the soul surfaces its deeper attachments. Hunger exposes dependency. Discomfort uncovers misplaced trust. Irritability reveals hidden control. Fasting does not create disordered desire; it unmasks it. And what God reveals, He desires to heal. The human heart was created with desire at its center. Desire itself is not sinful; it is sacred. Scripture reveals that God created humanity to hunger for Him: **"My soul thirsts for God, for the living God"** (Psalm 42:2). But in a fallen world, desire becomes fragmented. The heart learns to feed itself on lesser things—comfort, distraction, approval, entertainment, pleasure, control, achievement, and consumption. Over time, these substitutes dull spiritual hunger and weaken attentiveness to God. Fasting interrupts this cycle. It creates holy disruption. It asks the soul, with clarity and honesty: What do you truly hunger for?

When we fast, we allow the body to feel what the soul often ignores. Physical hunger becomes a teacher. Jesus reminds us that human life is not sustained by physical nourishment alone: **"Man shall not live by bread alone, but by every word that proceeds from the mouth of God"** (Matthew 4:4). Fasting confronts the illusion that constant satisfaction is necessary for peace. In fasting, the body learns restraint, and the soul relearns trust. Weakness becomes an invitation—not to despair, but to deeper reliance on God. Throughout Scripture, fasting accompanies moments of repentance, discernment, and renewal. God's people fasted when seeking direction (Acts 13:2–3), when repenting of sin (Joel 2:12), and when crying out for deliverance (Esther 4:16). Fasting slows the interior life and quiets competing appetites so the heart can attend to God. As external noise diminishes, spiritual sensitivity increases. Desire begins to reorder itself.

One of the most important works fasting accomplishes is exposing what competes with God for the heart's affection. Scripture warns that disordered desires wage war within the soul (James 4:1). When food, comfort, or routine is removed, the soul instinctively reaches for substitutes. Anxiety rises. Impatience surfaces. Control tightens. These reactions are not failures; they are revelations. God does not expose in order to condemn, but to restore. Fasting humbles the soul. It dismantles self-sufficiency and confronts the belief that we are sustained by what we consume or control. Scripture consistently links fasting with humility before God: **"Humble yourselves under the mighty hand of God"** (1 Peter 5:6). When hunger is embraced willingly, pride loses its footing. Dependence replaces self-reliance. In humility, grace flows freely, for **"God resists the proud, but gives grace to the humble"** (James 4:6).

At the same time, fasting retrains desire. What we feed grows stronger; what we deny weakens. When the appetite of the flesh is quieted, the appetite of the spirit awakens. Prayer deepens. Scripture speaks more clearly. Silence becomes less threatening and more inviting. The presence of God feels nearer, not because God has moved closer, but because the heart has become less divided. Fasting does not eliminate desire, it purifies it. It teaches the soul to long for what gives life rather than what merely distracts. This reordering of desire is why fasting is inseparable from prayer. Tobit 12:8-9 says, **"Prayer is good when accompanied by fasting, almsgiving and righteousness."** Fasting also loosens the grip of sin. Scripture teaches that self-control is a fruit of the Spirit (Galatians 5:22–23). When fasting trains restraint in legitimate desires, the will grows stronger against illegitimate ones. Over time, fasting weakens impulse-driven living and strengthens obedience. Freedom emerges—not through suppression, but through realignment of desire toward God. Yet fasting must always be rooted in love, not legalism. God never commanded fasting as a performance meant to impress Him. Jesus warns against fasting for human recognition in Matthew 6:16–18. True fasting is hidden, humble, and relational. It flows from desire for God, not from spiritual pride. God looks not at the length of the fast, but at the posture of the heart (Isaiah 58:4–9). Fasting may take many forms. While abstaining from food holds unique biblical significance, Scripture also calls believers to lay aside anything that entangles the heart: "**Therefore we also, since we are surrounded by so great a cloud of witnesses, let us lay aside every weight, and the sin which so easily ensnares us, and let us run with endurance the race that is set before us"** (Hebrews 12:1). Fasting from noise, distraction, or excess can likewise create space for God. The essence of fasting is not deprivation, but intentional emptying for the sake of deeper filling. As fasting becomes a rhythm rather than an occasional act, its fruit matures quietly. Desire clarifies, attachment loosens, discernment sharpens, dependence on God deepens, and the soul begins to recognize how often it reaches for substitutes when God is offering Himself. Gradually, the heart is retrained to hunger rightly.

In a culture of excess, fasting restores balance. In a world shaped by consumption, fasting teaches contentment: **"Godliness with contentment is great gain"** (1 Timothy 6:6). In lives driven by immediacy, fasting reintroduces patience and trust. It reminds the believer that true satisfaction flows not from fulfillment of every desire, but from communion with God. Ultimately, fasting is not about emptiness, it is about fullness. Scripture promises, **"Blessed are those who hunger and thirst for righteousness, for they shall be filled"** (Matthew 5:6). When desire is reordered toward God, everything else begins to fall into its proper place and spiritual life becomes integrated rather than divided.

The power of fasting lies not in what is removed, but in what is restored: a rightly ordered heart, a purified hunger, and a soul once again oriented toward God as its supreme good.

Closing Prayer

Eternal Father,

You know the desires of my heart— those that draw me toward You and those that quietly pull me away. I offer You my hunger, my weakness, and my dependence. Teach me to fast with wisdom, humility, and love. Reveal what rules my heart. Quiet my lesser appetites so my desire for You may grow strong. Reorder my loves until You alone are my greatest longing.

Lord, grant that fasting may free me rather than punish me—an emptying not for its own sake, but a sacred preparation for the fullness of Your presence. Holy Spirit, guide me in this discipline. Let every fast draw me closer to Christ, reshape my desires, and form within me a heart that hungers first and always for God.

In Jesus' name, Amen.

CHAPTER FIFTEEN

MAKING JESUS KNOWN — THE GREAT COMMISSION

S PIRITUAL FORMATION DOES NOT END in inward transformation alone. What God forms within the soul must eventually flow outward into witness. The journey of stillness, surrender, Scripture, fasting, sacramental union, and depth is never meant to terminate in private holiness. It is meant to culminate in love made visible. The formed life becomes a sent life. To know Christ truly is to be drawn into His mission—to make Him known. At the close of His earthly ministry, Jesus did not give His disciples a set of optional suggestions or inspirational ideals. He gave them a commission—a sending rooted in divine authority and eternal purpose. **"All authority in heaven and on earth has been given to Me"** (Matthew 28:18), He declared. And on the foundation of that authority, He spoke words that continue to shape the identity of the Church: **"Go therefore and make disciples of all nations, baptizing them in the name of the Father and of the Son and of the Holy Spirit, teaching them to observe all that I have commanded you. And behold, I am with you always, to the end of the age"** (Matthew 28:19–20).

The Great Commission is not merely a task assigned to especially gifted believers; it is the natural overflow of a life transformed by Christ. It is not a program to be implemented, but a posture to be embodied. Those who have encountered Jesus are sent to bear witness to Him—not primarily through argument or strategy, but through lives shaped by His presence and truth. At the heart of the Great Commission is authority—not human authority, but Christ's. The command to "go" is not limited to physical relocation. While some are called to cross borders, all are called to cross thresholds—to live intentionally as disciples wherever God has placed them. Going means carrying Christ into ordinary spaces: homes, workplaces, neighborhoods, relationships, and routines. It means recognizing that no moment is spiritually neutral. The Great Commission transforms daily life into sacred mission. Where the disciple goes, Christ desires to be revealed. Jesus grounds the mission in His sovereignty. He does not send His followers into the world uncertain or unsupported, He sends them with the assurance that He reigns. This means that the work of witnessing does not depend on human persuasion, cultural acceptance, or personal strength. It rests on the lordship of Christ Himself.

The Church does not advance the Gospel by force or fear, but by fidelity to the One who holds all things together. Saint Paul makes this unmistakable in Romans 10:13–15, where he unfolds the logic of salvation with sobering clarity: **"Everyone who calls on the name of the Lord will be saved."** This is the promise of God's mercy. But Paul immediately presses deeper: **"How then will they call on Him in whom they have not believed? And how are they to believe in Him of whom they have never heard? And how are they to hear without someone preaching? And how are they to preach unless they are sent? As it is written: How beautiful are the feet of those who preach the gospel of peace, Who bring glad tidings of good things!"** (Romans 10:13–15). In these words, Paul reveals a sacred chain of grace. Salvation begins with calling on the Lord, but calling requires belief; belief requires hearing; hearing requires proclamation; and proclamation requires sending. God, in His wisdom, has chosen to make His saving love known through human voices and faithful lives. The Gospel is God's power, yet He entrusts its announcement to His people. This does not diminish God's sovereignty—it magnifies His mercy. He allows redeemed sinners to participate in the work of redemption. This passage clarifies an essential truth about the Great Commission: making Jesus known is not optional silence cloaked in good intentions. Love speaks. Compassion proclaims. Faith bears witness. While a Christian life must always be lived before it is spoken, Scripture makes clear that witnessing cannot remain wordless. Presence without proclamation can become ambiguous; proclamation without presence can become hollow. God weaves both together. Lives shaped by Christ give credibility to words spoken about Christ, and words spoken about Christ give clarity to the meaning of lives transformed by Him.

The Great Commission calls believers not only to speak of Christ, but to reflect Him—to embody His character so that others encounter the Gospel through a living witness. Saint Paul understood this deeply when he wrote, **"I am not ashamed of the gospel, for it is the power of God for salvation to everyone who believes"** (Romans 1:16). Paul does not describe the Gospel as mere philosophy or moral guidance, but as divine power. The Gospel is God's active work in the world—His power to rescue, restore, and redeem. To be unashamed of the Gospel is not to be loud or aggressive, but to be convinced. It is to trust that the message of Christ crucified and risen carries within itself the power to transform hearts. Shame, fear, and silence are constant temptations for the believer. The world often resists the claims of Christ. Cultural pressure encourages faith to remain private, hidden, or diluted. In such an environment, making Jesus known requires courage—not the courage of confrontation, but the courage of faithfulness. To be unashamed of the Gospel is to refuse to hide what has given you life. It is to allow gratitude to overcome fear. When the Gospel has truly transformed the soul, silence becomes unnatural. Yet Jesus Himself issued a sobering warning: **"Whoever is ashamed of Me and of My words in this adulterous and sinful generation, of him will the Son of Man be ashamed when He comes in His glory"** (Luke 9:26). These words are not meant to terrify, but to awaken. They reveal that allegiance to Christ is not merely internal; it is relational and public. To belong to Jesus is to acknowledge Him— to identify with Him even when it costs reputation, comfort, or acceptance. This warning invites honest self-examination. What silences us? Is it fear of rejection? Desire for approval? Attachment to comfort? Anxiety about misunderstanding? Making Jesus known does not depend on eloquence, charisma, or approval. It depends on fidelity to Christ. Christ does not ask His followers to defend Him aggressively, but to confess Him faithfully.

Fear is one of the greatest obstacles to making Jesus known. Yet Scripture reassures us that **"God has not given us a spirit of fear, but of power, love, and self-control"** (2 Timothy 1:7). The courage required for witnessing is not a personality trait; it is a gift of the Spirit. The Holy Spirit does not eliminate risk, but He strengthens love. And perfect love casts out fear (1 John 4:18). The tension between fear and faith is not new. The earliest disciples faced opposition, ridicule, persecution, and misunderstanding. Yet what enabled them to speak boldly was not self-confidence, but

73

conviction born of encounter. They had seen the risen Christ. They had been changed by Him. Witnessing flowed from relationship. The same remains true today. Mission without formation becomes activism; formation without mission becomes self-enclosed spirituality.

The Great Commission also calls believers to make disciples, not merely converts. Jesus commands His followers to teach others to observe all that He commanded (Matthew 28:20). This is slow, relational work. Discipleship unfolds over time through presence, patience, instruction, correction, encouragement, and shared life. Making Jesus known means inviting others not only to belief, but to belonging—to life in Christ and life within His Body. It is an investment of love, not a transaction of information. The Great Commission is not a call to dominance, but to service. Christ sends His disciples not as conquerors, but as servants. Witnessing is never coercive, it respects freedom, it listens, it loves, and it trusts the Holy Spirit to work in hearts beyond what words alone can accomplish. Our role is faithfulness; God's role is conversion. When this distinction is forgotten, witnessing becomes heavy and anxious. When it is remembered, witnessing becomes peaceful and joyful. The promise at the end of the Great Commission is perhaps its most consoling element: **"I am with you always."** (Matthew 28:20). Jesus does not send His disciples alone; His presence accompanies the mission. As the soul matures through formation, witnessing becomes more integrated. The believer no longer feels torn between contemplation and mission. Prayer deepens courage, scripture shapes speech, sacrament strengthens love, fasting purifies motive, depth stabilizes faith, and mission becomes the natural expression of a life rooted in Christ. The Great Commission becomes not an obligation imposed from outside, but a desire flowing from within.

Ultimately, making Jesus known is an act of love. Love speaks. Love shares. Love invites. Love risks misunderstanding for the sake of another's good. To withhold the Gospel out of fear is not humility; it is forgetfulness of the gift we have received. When we remember what Christ has done—how He sought us, forgave us, healed us, and gave us life—we find the courage to speak His name with reverence and joy. The world does not need louder Christians; it needs truer ones. It needs disciples whose lives have been quietly and deeply formed by Christ—people who carry His presence into ordinary spaces, who speak His truth with gentleness, who love without condition, and who remain faithful even when it costs them.

To make Jesus known is to allow your life to become a testimony. Not performance, but presence. Not an argument, but an invitation. And as you go—wherever God has placed you—you do not go alone. You go with Christ, under His authority, sustained by His presence, bearing witness to the One who is the life of the world.

Closing Prayer

Lord Jesus Christ,

You who possess all authority in heaven and on earth, I thank You for calling me not only to know You, but to bear witness to You. Forgive me for the moments I have been silent out of fear, hesitant out of pride, or distracted by comfort. Free my heart from shame and give me courage rooted in love. Form my life so deeply in You that my words and actions naturally point to Your truth. Teach me to make disciples not by force, but by faithfulness, humility, and love.

Holy Spirit, guide my witness. Give me discernment to know when to speak and when to listen. Let my life reflect the Gospel I proclaim. May I never be ashamed of the One who gave His life for me. Jesus, remain with me as You promised. Go before me, walk beside me, and work through me. May everything I am and everything I do make You known and glorify the Father.

Amen.

Sending Tone

You are sent not as one who has arrived, but as one who is being faithfully formed. You are sent not by your own readiness, but by Christ's authority and presence.

Go into the places God has already prepared—ordinary places, hidden places, and difficult places—carrying within you the life you have received. Let your faith be steady rather than loud, your witness gentle rather than forceful, and your obedience rooted in love.

Do not measure your faithfulness by visible outcomes. Trust that God works through what is offered in humility. Remain attentive to His presence, anchored in truth, and surrendered to His will.

Go as one who belongs to Christ.
Go as one accompanied by His Spirit.
Go as one whose life quietly makes Jesus known.

Benediction

May God who called you into stillness
now steady you in faith.

May Christ,
who has formed your heart through surrender,
Scripture, the sacraments, and communion,
continue to dwell within you
and shape your life into His likeness.

May the Holy Spirit,
who reordered your desires and strengthened your interior life,
send you forth with courage rooted in love
and faithfulness grounded in truth.

As you go into the world,
may your life bear quiet witness to the Gospel.
May your words be few but faithful,
your actions shaped by mercy,
and your love reflective of Christ Himself.

Go as one formed, not perfected;
sent, not abandoned;
loved, not alone.

And may the blessing of Almighty God,
the Father, and the Son, and the Holy Spirit,
rest upon you, remain with you,
and guide you always—
now and forever.

Amen.

Lectio Divina Guide

Praying Scripture on the Journey of Formation**

"Speak, Lord, for Your servant is listening." (1 Samuel 3:10)

Lectio Divina is not a method for studying Scripture, but a way of **encountering God through His Word**. It invites the reader to move slowly, attentively, and prayerfully—allowing Scripture not merely to inform the mind, but to shape the heart.

Each session below follows the classic fourfold rhythm:

1. **Lectio (Read)** – Listen to the Word
2. **Meditatio (Reflect)** – Receive the Word
3. **Oratio (Respond)** – Speak to God
4. **Contemplatio (Rest)** – Abide in God

Move gently. Do not rush. Let the Spirit lead.

Session 1: Stillness, Silence & Listening to God

Scripture:

- Psalm 46:10
- 1 Kings 19:11–13
- Luke 10:39–42

Lectio

Read the passage slowly. Notice any word or phrase that draws your attention. Do not analyze—simply listen.

Meditatio

Ask:

- What keeps my heart from stillness?
- Where am I being invited to listen rather than strive?

Oratio

Speak honestly to God about your distractions, restlessness, or desire for quiet.

Contemplatio

Sit in silence for several minutes. Rest in God's presence without words.

Session 2: Prayer & Communion with God

Scripture:

- Matthew 6:4–6
- Romans 8:26
- 1 Thessalonians 5:17

Lectio

Read the passage aloud if possible. Let the words settle.

Meditatio

Ask:

- How do I approach prayer—out of duty or desire?
- Where might God be inviting deeper intimacy?

Oratio

Offer God your longing for prayer, even if prayer feels difficult.

Contemplatio

Remain quietly before God, trusting the Spirit to pray within you.

Session 3: Scripture & the Living Word

Scripture:

- Deuteronomy 8:3
- Psalm 119:105
- Hebrews 4:12

Lectio

Read attentively. Notice how Scripture describes itself.

Meditatio

Ask:

- Do I approach Scripture as information or nourishment?
- What is God illuminating in my life right now?

Oratio

Ask God to make His Word living and active within you.

Contemplatio

Rest in gratitude for God's Word spoken personally to you.

Session 4: Surrender, Obedience & Trust

Scripture:

- Proverbs 3:5–6
- Luke 9:23
- Matthew 26:39

Lectio

Read slowly. Pay attention to Jesus' posture of surrender.

Meditatio

Ask:

- What am I holding tightly?
- Where am I resisting God's will?

Oratio

Name what you are struggling to surrender. Offer it gently to God.

Contemplatio

Remain with God in trust, even without resolution.

Session 5: Living in the Presence of God

Scripture:

- Acts 17:28
- Psalm 16:11
- John 15:4–5

Lectio

Read as if God is speaking directly to you.

Meditatio

Ask:

- Do I live as if God is near or distant?
- What would change if I truly abided in Him?

Oratio

Thank God for His nearness. Ask for awareness of His presence.

Contemplatio

Abide quietly, allowing God to be enough.

Session 6: The Holy Eucharist & Communion

Scripture:

- John 6:51–57
- 1 Corinthians 10:16–17

Lectio

Read prayerfully, especially if preparing for Mass.

Meditatio

Ask:

- What does it mean that Christ gives Himself to me?
- How does the Eucharist shape my life?

Oratio

Respond with gratitude, reverence, and longing for union.

Contemplatio

Rest in silent adoration, whether before the Eucharist or in prayer.

Session 7: Fasting & Reordering Desire

Scripture:

- Matthew 4:4
- Psalm 42:2
- Isaiah 58:6–9

Lectio

Read attentively. Let hunger imagery speak.

Meditatio

Ask:

- What do I turn to instead of God?
- What might God be reordering in my desires?

Oratio

Offer your longings, appetites, and attachments to God.

Contemplatio

Sit with God as your true satisfaction.

Session 8: Eternal Depth & Spiritual Maturity

Scripture:

- Psalm 1:3
- Colossians 3:2–3
- Philippians 1:6

Lectio

Read slowly. Picture the imagery of rootedness.

Meditatio

Ask:

- What kind of spiritual depth is God forming in me?
- Where am I being invited to grow patiently?

Oratio

Thank God for His ongoing work in your soul.

Contemplatio

Rest in trust that God will complete what He has begun.

Session 9: Mission & Making Jesus Known

Scripture:

- Matthew 28:18–20
- Romans 10:13–15
- Luke 9:26

Lectio

Read with openness to being sent.

Meditatio

Ask:

- Where is God sending me right now?
- What fear or hesitation do I need to surrender?

Oratio

Offer yourself again to God's mission.

Contemplatio

Rest in Christ's promise: *"I am with you always."*

Closing Prayer for Lectio Divina

Lord Jesus Christ,

Draw me into stillness,
that I may listen more than speak,
receive more than analyze,
and trust more than strive.

Form me through Your Word,
sustain me in Your presence,
and send me in Your love.

May my life be shaped by Scripture,
and may it bear witness to You.

Amen.

Thematic Scripture Index

Stillness, Silence & Listening to God

- Psalm 46:10
- Psalm 5:3
- 1 Kings 19:11–13
- Habakkuk 2:20
- Luke 10:39–42

Prayer & Communion with God

- Matthew 6:4–6
- Matthew 11:28
- Luke 11:9–13
- Romans 8:26
- 1 Thessalonians 5:17

Scripture & the Living Word

- Deuteronomy 8:3
- Psalm 119:105
- John 1:1–4
- John 6:63
- Hebrews 4:12

Formation of the Interior life

- Psalm 51:10
- Proverbs 4:23
- Romans 12:1–2
- 2 Corinthians 4:16–18
- Philippians 1:6

Renewal of the Mind & Spiritual Warfare

- Romans 12:2
- 2 Corinthians 10:3–5
- Philippians 4:8
- Ephesians 6:10–18

Suffering, Trials & Endurance

- Matthew 13:20–21
- Romans 8:18
- James 1:2–4
- 1 Peter 1:6–7
- 2 Corinthians 1:3–5

Surrender, Obedience & Trust

- Proverbs 3:5–6
- Luke 9:23
- Matthew 26:39
- Romans 12:1
- John 4:34

Living in the Presence of God

- Genesis 17:1
- Acts 17:28
- Psalm 16:11
- Isaiah 26:3
- John 15:4–5

The Holy Eucharist & Communion

- Matthew 26:26–28
- Luke 22:19–20
- John 6:51–57
- 1 Corinthians 10:16–17
- 1 Corinthians 11:23–29

The Blessed Virgin Mary & Intercession

- Luke 1:38, 46–48
- John 2:3–5
- John 19:25–27
- Acts 1:14
- Revelation 12:1

Fasting & Reordering Desire

- Matthew 4:1–4
- Matthew 6:16–18
- Psalm 42:2
- Joel 2:12
- Isaiah 58:6–9

Eternal Depth & Spiritual Maturity

- Psalm 1:3
- Colossians 3:2–3
- Hebrews 5:12–14
- Philippians 2:15
- John 15:16

Love, Holiness & the Fruit of the Spirit

- 1 Corinthians 13:1–13
- Galatians 5:22–23
- John 13:34–35
- 1 John 4:7–12

Mission, Witness & the Great Commission

- Matthew 28:18–20
- Romans 1:16
- Romans 10:13–15
- Luke 9:26
- Acts 1:8

Hope, Glory & Eternal Life

- John 11:25
- Romans 8:18
- Revelation 19:9
- Revelation 21:1–4

ABOUT THE PUBLISHER

Quiet Watch Publishing was founded to serve readers seeking depth, reverence, and spiritual clarity in an age marked by distraction and haste. Its mission is to publish works that call the Christian soul to vigilance, interior honesty, and faithful response to grace—without sensationalism, polemic, or dilution of truth.

The titles released under Quiet Watch Publishing are intentionally contemplative in nature. They are written not for hurried consumption, but for careful reading, prayerful reflection, and sustained engagement. Drawing from Sacred Scripture and the historic Christian tradition, these works aim to restore seriousness to questions often treated casually, and hope to themes frequently reduced to sentiment.

Quiet Watch Publishing operates quietly by design. Its focus is not on authorial prominence or cultural relevance, but on fidelity—to the Gospel, to the Church's wisdom, and to the dignity of the reader's conscience. The press exists to support works that invite conversion rather than comfort, depth rather than distraction, and truth spoken in charity rather than fear.

www.ingramcontent.com/pod-product-compliance
Lightning Source LLC
Chambersburg PA
CBHW030603130626
46552CB00006B/2646

* 9 7 9 8 9 9 4 5 3 2 6 0 7 *